CONTENTS

List of Figures v

Introduction... vii

CHAPTER 1
Framing the Research Question 1

CHAPTER 2
Identifying and Selecting the Methodology 19

CHAPTER 3
Conducting Qualitative Research on College Student Transitions 41

CHAPTER 4
Conducting Quantitative Research on College Student Transitions 63

CHAPTER 5
Publishing Results and Disseminating Findings 85

APPENDIX A
Additional Resources 103

APPENDIX B
Journal of The First-Year Experience & Students in Transition
Review Form.. 105

References.. 109

Index.. 121

CRAFTING AND CONDUCTING RESEARCH ON
STUDENT TRANSITIONS

Jean M. Henscheid and Jennifer R. Keup

NATIONAL RESOURCE CENTER

FIRST-YEAR EXPERIENCE® AND STUDENTS IN TRANSITION
UNIVERSITY OF SOUTH CAROLINA

Cite as:

Henscheid, J. M., & Keup, J. R. (2011). *Crafting and conducting research on student transitions*. Columbia, SC: University of South Carolina, National Resource Center for The First-Year Experience and Students in Transition.

Production Staff for the National Resource Center:
Project Manager   Dottie Weigel, Editor
Design and Production   Shana Bertetto, Graphic Artist

Additional copies of this book may be obtained from the National Resource Center for The First-Year Experience and Students in Transition, University of South Carolina, 1728 College Street, Columbia, SC 29208. Telephone (803) 777-6229. Fax (803) 777-4699.

Library of Congress Cataloging-in-Publication Data
Henscheid, Jean M.
  Crafting and conducting research on student transitions / by Jean M. Henscheid and Jennifer R. Keup.
      p. cm.
  Includes bibliographical references.
  ISBN 978-1-889271-78-1
  1. College students--United States--Research--Methodology. 2. College freshmen--United States--Research--Methodology. 3. College graduates--United States--Research--Methodology. 4. School-to-work transition--United States--Research--Methodology. I. Keup, Jennifer R. II. Title.
  LB3605.H44 2011
  378.1'980973--dc23
                  2011019224

LIST OF FIGURES

Figure 2.1   Myths About Research Methodologies 21

Figure 2.2   Comparison of Qualitative and Quantitative
              Methodology 26

Figure 2.3   Methodological Categories for Verbs Used in
              Research Questions on Student Transitions 36

Introduction

Vestiges of support for new students in higher education can be found as early as the 16th century. For example, mentorship programs for new students date back to the era of colonial colleges; accounts of academic advising programs tailored for the needs of first-year students can be found as early as the 1700s, and the first extended orientation courses (i.e., first-year seminars) date back to approximately 1880. However, the organized attempt to provide a comprehensive and integrated transition experience for first-year students emerged in the 1970s. Thus, what higher education recognizes as the modern first-year experience and students in transition movement is only decades, rather than centuries, old and a relatively new addition to the study and practice of higher education.

In order to fully support the growing first-year experience movement on a national scale, the National Resource Center for The First-Year Experience and Students in Transition was established in 1987 and has supported and advanced the first-year experience movement and the study of higher education through conferences, online resources, and networking activities. In an effort to fill a void in the literature base for the emerging field of the first-year experience and students in transition, the National Resource Center also collaborated with prominent scholars, practitioners, and graduate students in higher education to develop a full complement of publications and a research agenda on student transitions in postsecondary education. Further, in 1989 the National Resource Center founded a scholarly, peer-refereed journal titled the *Journal of The First-Year Experience & Students in Transition*[1] as a vehicle for new research in this emerging subspecialty of higher education.

In these collaborative efforts to serve as a clearinghouse for existing research on the topic of student transitions and success in postsecondary education as well as to chart a research agenda in this area, the staff and affiliates of the Center have often provided research counsel. The purpose

---

[1] Originally published as the *Journal of The Freshman Year Experience*, the journal has since changed its name twice to reflect its expanding mission.

of this publication is to draw from many years of experience supporting professionals who are dedicated to the study and service of students in transition and to contribute to the larger body of literature in higher education. It is similar in purpose to a previous volume published on this topic by the Center in its purpose "to guide experienced and inexperienced researchers through the entire process, from selecting a topic to disseminating the research results" (Fidler & Henscheid, 2001, p. 5). To set the stage for this book, it is important that the authors adequately introduce the purposes and goals of the content contained herein, which we offer in our answers to the fundamental Ws of investigation: Who, What, When, Where, and Why. Answers to these questions effectively lead to the content of this volume and provide a comprehensive answer to the How question.

Who?

The Who question really has two significant answers with respect to this book. The first answer addresses the question, Who is the subject of the research? Topics and subjects of research are truly infinite so some parameters were needed for this volume. The primary focus of the research designs, considerations, and examples of this book are college students, particularly those who are undergoing transitions, such as typically experienced in the first year of college, as a sophomore, in transferring to a new institution, and upon graduation. While research on the college student experience can include studies of faculty, curricula, policy, governance structures, and even parents, the preponderance of work on college student transitions is still focused on the student as the primary unit of observation. Further, although student transition is also inclusive of new graduate students, the dearth of literature on this newly recognized point of transition necessitated a focus on the undergraduate experience in this volume. However, it should be noted that the tactics, methods, and techniques described in this book are transferable to the design and execution of research studies on new graduate students as well as other transition points not explicitly mentioned.

The second Who question asks, Who is a researcher? The authors believe that anyone can conduct research. Of course, specific training, degrees, predispositions, and interests may make the research process easier or more accessible. However, neither a doctorate nor intimate understanding of critical theory nor advanced knowledge of statistical software packages are necessary to conduct research on the transition experiences of college students. All that is required is intellectual curiosity, a commitment to the field of higher education, and a willingness to learn and collaborate. In fact, many people are unwittingly becoming researchers in our field due to demands for increased accountability in higher education as well as the development of the first-year experience and students in transition as a subspecialty of higher education. This book embraces all educators as scholars and assumes their potential to engage in the research process.

What?

Research is a structured process of inquiry that draws upon existing knowledge and theory to advance general understanding or impact practices in the field at large. There are generally two kinds of research: basic and applied. Basic research "is carried out primarily to test a theory" with little or no emphasis on practical implications or application; whereas, applied research is conducted to address a real-world issue (Bordens & Abbott, 1991, p. G-2). Although both are certainly possible in higher education, studies of college students in transition tend to be more in line with applied research. In fact, this symbiotic connection between research and practice is a core commitment of the National Resource Center and is evident in its activities to support scholarly practice as well as applied research.

As with many definitional elements, it is almost easier to explain what research is not than what it is. The most fundamental distinction of this variety for the current volume is the differentiation of assessment from research. Given the demand for greater accountability in higher education, institutional and program assessment activities have grown exponentially. However, it is important to understand that assessment is a distinctly different enterprise than research. The scope of assessment is typically narrower than research as its focus is almost uniformly institution specific with respect to the population of interest and the application of findings. Further, research is well situated within the theoretical and empirical literature on a topic while assessment is generally associated with learning outcomes within a very specific program or institutional context. The line between research and assessment can become very blurry, especially as research may be conducted with institution-specific samples and the learning outcomes associated with assessment activities may be very broad in scope. However, the primary difference is in the goals of each: "research focuses on the creation of new knowledge, testing an experimental hypothesis, or documenting new knowledge" while assessment focuses on "program accountability, program management, or decision-making and budget" (McGillin, 2003, para. 3).

When?

The most apt issue to address with respect to the When question is really, Why now? This book represents the third iteration of a research primer on this topic. The first was published in 1992, and a revised edition was released in 2001. During that time, the first-year experience and students in transition movement has matured and generated significant research on the transition and success experiences of undergraduates. Since those early primers, several national research projects—National Survey of Student Engagement (NSSE), the Your First College Year (YFCY) survey, program assessment by Educational Benchmarking Inc., and the Wabash National Study of Liberal Arts Education—were developed and conducted to measure change during college. These studies have helped generate new lines of inquiry regarding the undergraduate experience and created tools and data sources that advance our understanding of college student learning, development, and success.

Also during this time, qualitative inquiry in higher education has continued to expand on both the institutional and national levels. National studies using student interviews and institutional case studies have been the foundation of ground-breaking work on the college student experience, including studies of student self-authorship (Baxter Magolda, 2009), defining effective practices in undergraduate education (Kuh, Kinzie, Schuh, Whitt, & Associates, 2005), and identifying criteria for excellence in the first year of college (Barefoot et al., 2005).

This research productivity in the field of higher education has created a momentum that makes it a very exciting time to engage in scholarly work on the experiences of college students. As research is fundamentally an iterative process, previous work generates new questions to address and fresh pathways of inquiry to pursue. When coupled with the emergence of new methods, data sources, student populations, and institutional contexts, it is apparent that we are currently entering what may someday be remembered as a golden age of research on student learning and success in higher education.

Where?

In some ways this question may appear to have the most obvious answer. Where does one conduct research on college student transitions and success? At the college, of course! Yet, the evolution of higher education has made the notion of where student transition, learning, and success takes place much more complex.

First, the very definition of higher education institutions has broadened over the years with greater proportions of students starting their college experiences in community colleges, for-profit campuses, and with online education providers. Additionally, the traditional notion of one student engaging with one educational institution at a time has also been challenged by increasing transfer pathways, formal dual-enrollment programs, and students swirling among many institutions in pursuit of their educational requirements. This complexity is especially true for research on the first-year experience and students in transition as transition itself includes a move from one educational environment to another. As such, the Where of research can include new and multiple higher education contexts.

Second, the boundaries within educational environments are also blurring with respect to the location of students' education and development. Historically, it was perceived that the classroom was the domain of cognitive learning, and the cocurriculum was the location for affective and interpersonal development. In recent decades, these traditional boundaries have been challenged by scholars and practitioners—many in the first-year experience and students in transition fields—so that student learning and development is more integrated across different segments of the campus and between different student experiences. Further, students' higher education experiences are including other life domains outside of the campus as illustrated by student employment, family responsibilities, study abroad, and internships. In fact, the expansion of the notion of where education takes place is a driving force behind the newest wave of research questions about students' educational experiences, transition, and success.

Why?

As mentioned earlier, the first-year experience and students in transition area of higher education is a relatively new subspecialty and focus of research. It is critical that new research help this field evolve and develop. Existing theories of student development, adjustment, and persistence need to be tested within the context of what we now know about college student transitions as critical points in the educational pipeline. Further, new theory is needed that directly addresses the unique learning and development opportunities that occur during points of transition in students' college career.

Additional research is necessary to learn more about the needs and experiences of new students and help support their success. While the number of new students is expected to remain fairly constant over the next several decades, national data indicate that the composition of future cohorts of undergraduates will be more diverse in their background, needs, and expectations than ever before. (e.g., Aud et al., 2011; Crissman Ishler, 2005; Western Interstate Commission for Higher Education, 2008). Further, trends in higher education, including enhanced technology, different sectors of higher education such as for-profit colleges, and declining resources, create a set of conditions in which educators can address emerging issues for college students as well as perennial concerns for undergraduate education. In order to meet the challenges and seize the opportunities that these trends are sure to provide, it is imperative that relevant information and current research be used to help educators learn from one another and inform decisions in higher education.

Organizational Overview

The remainder of this volume will address the How question of research. The book opens in chapter 1 with a discussion of how to develop the framework to take a general interest or idea about the college student experience and shape it into a question that grounds a research study. The process of building the scaffolding for a study is heavily informed by theory and previous research, which are investigated via a thorough literature review on the topic of interest. Chapter 1 provides a roadmap to understanding the role of theory and conducting a literature review in the process of identifying, refining, and conducting a research study on the undergraduate experience in higher education.

Chapter 2 continues the discussion of the research process by introducing the concept of methodology and its role in the development and execution of high-quality research on the undergraduate student experience. More specifically, characteristics of qualitative, quantitative, and mixed methodologies are outlined as well as general points of consideration in the selection of the appropriate methodology for a research study. The chapters that follow build upon the foundation of methodology introduced in chapter 2 and explore the various approaches and tactics for conducting qualitative (chapter 3) and quantitative (chapter 4) research in higher education.

This volume concludes with chapter 5, which is dedicated to the final phase of research: disseminating the findings via presentations, reports, and publication. Sharing the outcome of the research process is a critical step in advancing the knowledge of the undergraduate student experience and informing practice in higher education. Further, closing the feedback loop on a study by disseminating results and discussing limitations that were discovered as a part of that process helps generate new lines of inquiry, thereby advancing the higher education research agenda at large.

It is necessary to state one important qualification regarding the use of this book. The authors have intended to provide an introduction to research on undergraduate student transitions. As such, this text serves as a general overview of the research process and not a comprehensive source on research questions, designs, techniques, and dissemination channels. It is not intended as a substitute for the numerous publications that offer more in-depth discussions of these topics. Instead, this book is designed to be a starting point and a companion guide for other resources. Anyone engaging in a study of the college student experience is advised to complement this book with several other publications and resources to support their research enterprise. Our hope is that readers will find this a useful roadmap for the research journey to explore, identify, and apply new knowledge on the college student experience.

CHAPTER 1
FRAMING THE RESEARCH QUESTION

Three decades ago, Robert Pace published *Measuring Outcomes of College: Fifty Years of Findings and Recommendations for the Future* (1979), a look at research activity in higher education dating back to the early years of the 20th century. Pace and his successors in researching and documenting the college student experience have built what is today a rich, and often overwhelming, literature base on this topic. In this context, today's researchers are tasked with formulating and studying compelling questions and making important contributions to educational theory and practice. With so much material to build upon, what questions are left to be asked about the college student experience and, for the purposes of this book in particular, about students in transition? Where does one find what has already been said about these topics?

This chapter provides some of the answers. It will help researchers distinguish between what motivates a study (the research interest and topic) and what shapes a study (the research question and problem). We will also examine the role of theory in asking and answering important research questions and offer assistance on conducting efficient literature reviews on the contexts, substance, and methodologies pertinent to studying students in transition. While Pace and others have been examining the college student experience for a century, research on college student transitions is newer—dating back just 30 years. There are still hundreds of important questions to be asked and answered on this broad topic, and with an ever-changing educational landscape, the supply of questions is not likely to run out.

Interests, Topics, Questions, and Problems

Successful studies begin with the researcher's interest, defined by Booth, Colomb, and Williams (1995), as "a general area of inquiry" (p. 36). Sophomores, summer bridge programs, capstone courses, or graduate students are interest areas related to studying students in transition that are good places to start but too broad to serve as the basis for designing and conducting research projects. Narrower topics with more research potential typically include nouns and verbs. Using the interests above, finer grained researchable topics might include: the role of academic advising in sophomore success, the Latina experience of a science-technology-engineering-math summer bridge program, the development of critical thinking among seniors in an interdisciplinary capstone course, or the reasons for choosing graduate school among English majors. The advantage of a narrow topic is that the researcher can more easily recognize "gaps, inconsistencies, and puzzles" (Booth et al., p. 38) that can be studied than he or she could if using an interest area or broad topic. Narrowing also helps to eventually turn the topic into a research question. A far-from-complete list of interest areas and topics related to college student transitions currently under scrutiny by researchers includes dual enrollment (i.e., students receiving simultaneous high school and college credit), enrollment processes and academic success rates of underrepresented populations (i.e., adults, Native Americans, Latinos, African Americans, students with disabilities, undocumented immigrants), college experiences of military veterans, the kindergarten-through-college (K-16) system, redefinitions of academic success, and the role of online social networking and other computer technologies on the student experience. These are topics suitable for formulation into research questions.

Once the researchable topic has been determined, the next step in designing a study is to develop a research question: that is, what the researcher and others must know or understand about a topic but currently do not know or understand. Formulating a research question includes applying Who, What, Where, When, Why, and How questions to a topic area. For example, who, if any, among students in an interdisciplinary capstone course report developing critical thinking skills, and why do they believe it was developed? What is the role of academic advising in sophomore success? Where do English majors from public versus private institutions attend graduate school, and why do they attend? When do these students choose to attend graduate school? How do Latinas experience a science-technology-engineering-math summer bridge program? Subjecting a topic to these types of questions is intended to stimulate and refine one's thinking but is unlikely to result in a polished research question. The question typically develops as a result of the literature review, as described below. Applying these traditional W questions to the research topic may also aid in the identification of a research problem (i.e., the case built by the researcher that answering the research question is essential not only to themselves but to others in the field). The research question is an important query posed about a topic. The research problem takes this one step further by demonstrating that the condition of not knowing the answer to the question is unacceptable to the researcher and to others. Formulating both is an iterative process between posing questions and conducting the literature review on what knowledge already exists.

The Role of Theory

As a social science, educational research is typically intended to either generate a new theory or to confirm or refute an existing theory. Theory is defined as "an explanation or explanatory system that discusses how a phenomenon operates and why it operates as it does" (Johnson & Christensen, 2008, p. 63). In research on issues related to students in transition, studies are conducted to describe and explain how the environments around these students (i.e., institutions, educational interventions, social environments) operate; how the students themselves or those who interact with them function under those conditions; and the consequences or outcomes for the students, faculty, staff, institution, or other individuals or entities related to student transitions. When a study is conducted to generate a theory from data that are collected first, it is considered inductive or exploratory and is most often carried out by a qualitative researcher. When a study is designed to confirm or refute a theory (or test a hypothesis), it is considered deductive or confirmatory and is most often conducted by a quantitative researcher. As Johnson and Christensen note, qualitative and quantitative researchers emphasize different aspects of the same cycle to conduct their research:

Quantitative researchers emphasize movement from theory to hypotheses to data to conclusions (i.e., the "logic of justification"), and qualitative researchers emphasize movement directly from observations and data to descriptions and patterns, and, sometimes, to theory generation (i.e., the "logic of discovery"). (p. 19)

As the researcher formulates a preliminary research question and reviews the literature, he or she will consider whether the research question is related to the lack of an existing explanation for the phenomenon of interest (the theory) or to the need to test someone else's explanation of the phenomenon. Through this process, the researcher determines whether a qualitative or quantitative study (or one combining both methodologies) should be conducted. The Documenting Effective Educational Practice (DEEP) project serves as a good example of the use of both theory-generating (inductive) and theory-confirming (deductive) approaches. Following several years of administration of the National Survey of Student Engagement (NSSE), researchers identified a group of four-year institutions where student scores on the NSSE, which measures student engagement, were better than predicted based on institutional profiles. The DEEP project was undertaken to explore and explain what conditions existed at these institutions that may positively impact (or at least correlate with) better-than-expected student engagement. The researchers identified the existence of four conditions: (a) leadership, (b) partnerships between academic and student affairs personnel, (c) student agency, and (d) what the team defined as "the power of one" (Kinzie & Kuh, 2004, p. 3). Presence of these conditions can be viewed as a theory generated by the researchers now testable at other institutions. New deductive (theory confirming) research can now be designed to determine whether these conditions exist at other institutions. One follow-up quantitative study, for example, might employ a survey administered to a large number of institutions with findings subjected to statistical analysis. Several other examples of studies conducted to generate or test theories related to students in transition are offered in upcoming chapters on the use of qualitative and quantitative research methods.

Current Theories on Students in Transition

From its inception, the National Resource Center for The First-Year Experience and Students in Transition has focused its attention on the liminal condition of college students moving from one set of circumstances to another (i.e., transition) in the belief that change poses particular challenges to students and is, thus, of particular research interest. Researchers at the National Resource Center and others who study college student transitions work to understand what happens during these transitions and how that knowledge can inform the design of what Kuh and his colleagues (2005, 2010) refer to as high-impact, formal and informal, learning experiences and services for students. Interest in moments of student transition has prompted researchers and practitioners to draw on cross-disciplinary bodies of research and practices in and outside of education to help make sense of them.

William Bridges (1980), author of 10 books on the subject of personal and organizational transitions, offers a starting point for understanding the topic. Bridges defines transition as "...the natural process of disorientation and reorientation that marks the turning point of the path of growth... [T]he key times in the natural process of self-renewal" (p. 5). He posits that all transitions involve three stages, including (a) endings, which he suggests is often confused with finality; (b) the neutral zone (i.e., a time of disorientation and disconnection that may seem unproductive); and (c) the new beginning (i.e., new activities that offer a path to the future).

While Bridges uses a humanistic psychologist's perspective to explain transitions in a variety of contexts, others employ perspectives from across the spectrum of academic disciplines, including those from other social sciences, natural and physical sciences, and the humanities. Many such viewpoints have been used to try to explain college preparation and access and other intense periods in the college student experience with bearing on persistence (e.g., the first year, academic major changes, transfer between schools, imminent graduation, and personal tragedies). Cross-disciplinary viewpoints have also been used to explore the outcomes of these transitional periods and to generate, adapt, or confirm theories about them. Tinto's theory of social integration (1987, 1994) is one of the most widely known and oft-tested theories about student persistence, but dozens more exist about this and other transitions, as either original theories or as adaptation of existing theories—Tinto's theory is actually an adaptation of Durkheim's (1951) study of suicide.

What follow are examples of approaches used by scholars published in the *Journal of The First-Year Experience and Students in Transition* to understand student transition: Fuertes, Sedlacek, Roger, and Mohr's (2000) correlates of universal-diverse orientation among first-year university students; Brower's (1997) striving for future-self as an information management strategy in the transition to college; Schwitzer, Ancis, and Griffin's (1998) model of African American students' social adjustment; Richardson and Sullivan's (1994) motivation-related noncognitive factors related to the success of academically underprepared first-year students, and Franklin's (2000) exploration of life role complexity as a force in learning communities. Over the years, frameworks for understanding student transitions have been drawn from a variety of theories, including social structural, developmental, cognitive, social learning, adolescent identity, planned behavior, prosocial reasoning and behavior, emerging adulthood, agency, sociohistorical, sociocultural, and implicit intelligence. There is still much left to learn from adapting and applying existing theories to important moments in the lives of college students. Where to go to discover these existing theories and to formulate an original research question about student transitions is the purpose of the next section.

The Literature Review

Once the preliminary research question and problem have been identified and early ideas about the theory to be generated or tested have been formulated, the next step in the research process is learning what knowledge already exists through reading and summarizing previous relevant work. Researchers on college student transitions generally conduct a review of literature in three areas: (a) higher education and its larger context, (b) the specific college student transition experience under consideration, and (c) research methodologies appropriate to answering the research question. During reviews of the literature, gaps in the knowledge base, either at the contextual, substantive, or methodological level, will help the researcher fine tune the research question and clarify the research problem that needs to be addressed. In research on college student transitions, books and journal articles are a good place to begin a literature review. All are available at little to no cost in college and university libraries, through interlibrary loan; in academic departments or units responsible for undergraduate education; or through WorldCat, an online database that searches the catalogs of 36,000 libraries worldwide. Access to WorldCat and all other databases (described in greater detail below) is available through nearly every college and university library. If print resources are not locally available, it may be appropriate to suggest that the library or department acquire them for ready access during a research project. Researchers may also wish to purchase some of these publications for their own personal libraries. Books, journals, and other print materials are important tools of the educational trade and are a good investment for both researchers and practitioners. According to one seasoned university librarian (R. Attebury, personal communication, May 26, 2010), a common mistake researchers make is bypassing print materials, particularly books, and heading directly to online-only resources to launch their literature reviews. Book-length treatments continue to be the researcher's best source for a broad overview of any topic and typically include the most exhaustive review of literature available. Attebury suggests first familiarizing oneself with one's own local library, its books and other holdings, before heading to online-only resources.

Accessing and Using Research Databases

Whether seeking online-only or print materials from the local library or from around the world, researchers now conduct all literature searches through online databases. Three types of databases are currently available to the researcher conducting a review of literature on topics in higher education: (a) indexing, (b) abstracting, and (c) full-text. Indexing databases replicate traditional print indices and provide full citation information on a source. They are increasingly rare but may still appear in a search. Abstracting databases provide the full citation information and typically the original abstract written for the source and subject or keywords that have been assigned to the source to aid further searching. Both indexing and abstracting databases will often provide information for obtaining full-text documents. Full-text databases provide the full citation, abstract, subject or keywords, and typically a portable document format (PDF) or hypertext markup language (HTML) version of the entire document. The level of subscription an institution or individual has may also determine whether full text is accessible to the user. Two of the most widely available databases for higher education researchers, the Education Resource Information Center (ERIC) and the Database of Research in International Education, are open source (i.e., free and available without subscription) while others require a subscription. Any researcher with an affiliation to a college or university or local library has free access to many of these subscription databases, and some state library commissions provide access to them for state residents. Listed and briefly described below are the most relevant databases for researching topics related to college students in transition.

Database of Research in International Education, an open-source, searchable database, contains details of nearly 8,000 books, articles, conference papers and reports on various aspects of international education from publishers in Australia and beyond. The database houses material published from 1990 onwards, a period of major change in education systems and services.

EdResearch Online is a database of more than 30,400 articles from some 200 Australian education journals. These records are from the Australian Education Index.

Education Abstracts, produced by the H. W. Wilson Company, indexes and abstracts articles from more than 680 periodicals and yearbooks, with indexing dating back to 1983 and abstracts dating back to 1994. Books on education published after 1995 are also indexed. Subjects covered include adult education, continuing education, library science, literacy standards, multicultural or ethnic education, teaching methods, and more.

Education Full Text (or Education Index) is maintained by in-house librarians and subject specialists. Database content includes full text of articles from more than 350 journals dating from 1996, 12 years of text from *Wilson Library Bulletin*, indexing of more than 770 periodicals dating back to 1983, more than 50 journals dedicated to special education, and more than 100,000 controlled and cross-referenced names of educational tests.

Education Index Retrospective (1929-1983) offers more than a half century of coverage with citations to some 850,000 articles, including book reviews. The database is used to track trends in education and changes in society and cultural attitudes. It is also valuable for sociological, legal, and historical studies.

Education Research Complete, from EBSCO Publishing, is the world's largest collection of full-text education journals, covering curriculum and instruction, administration, policy, funding, and related social issues. The database provides indexing and abstracts for more than 2,100 journals, as well as full text for nearly 1,300 journals, more than 550 books and monographs, and numerous education-related conference papers.

*Educational Administration Abstracts (*formerly Educational Abstracts), from EBSCO Publishing, includes bibliographic records covering areas related to educational administration, including educational leadership, educational management, educational research, and other areas of relevance to the discipline. The index contains more than 66,000 records, selected from *Educational Administration Quarterly, Journal of Educational Administration, The Review of Higher Education,* and similar sources. EBSCO has digitized the full archive of this index, including coverage dating back to 1966.

Educational Research Abstracts (ERA) Online is a database comprising abstracts addressing current international research in education. ERA contains links to the full-text, online versions of articles where possible and includes 50,000 abstracts that are updated monthly. ERA also includes 700 scanned journals and an archive dating from 1995. It is primarily aimed at researchers, students studying all fields of education, and academic practitioners. Abstracts are categorized for the following: child development, educational management, educational technology, health education, higher education, literacy, multicultural education, sociology of education, special needs, and technical education and training.

Educational Technology Abstracts, an international abstracting service, is designed to assist teachers, educational technologists, and instructional designers identify important, recently published material in the field of the technology of education and training. The database covers all aspects of educational technology: instructional design and educational planning; teaching methods, including open learning, games, and simulations; instructional media, such as computers, educational television, interactive video, and hypermedia; instructional resources, including libraries, learning laboratories, and audio-visual resources; learning, including study skills, learning theories, motivation, and problem solving; and issues of assessment and evaluation. It is also part of ERA Online. In 2010, there were 10,915 records in the database.

The Education Resource Information Center (ERIC) provides access to education literature and resources through its Current Index of Journals in Education and Resources in Education Index. In 2010, ERIC contained more than 1,300,000 records and links to more than 323,000 full-text documents dating back to 1966.

Higher Education Abstracts (formerly College Student Personnel Abstracts), published by The Claremont Graduate University, is a quarterly compilation of abstracts of journal articles, research reports, and books pertaining to college students, faculty, administrators, and related topics in higher education. It covers more than 200 journals in the fields of education, computer sciences, management, psychology, sociology, and law; papers read at meetings of major education and social sciences conferences; books published by all major higher education publishers; and research reports issued by professional organizations, government agencies, and foundations.

Professional Development Collection, from EBSCO Publishing, is a compilation of electronic information for educators, librarians and researchers, with a focus on children's health and development and pedagogical theory and practice. The database includes full text for *The Chronicle of Higher Education, Educational Leadership, Journal of Education, The Journal of Higher Education, Theory Into Practice*, and nearly 520 other education journals. This database also contains more than 200 educational reports.

Research Into Higher Education Abstracts is the British equivalent to Higher Education Abstracts. This title is included in ERA Online. In 2010, there were 20,766 records in the database.

Social Sciences Citation Index, retrieved via Web of Science, provides researchers, administrators, faculty, and students with access to the bibliographic and citation information needed to find research data, analyze trends, and share findings. The database focuses on data from approximately 2,500 of the world's leading social sciences journals across 50 disciplines.

Sociology of Education Abstracts, founded in 1965, is a resource for those involved in research and teaching from around the world with a focus on the sociological study of education. This database is included in ERA Online. In 2010, there were 12,540 records in the database.

Special Educational Needs Abstracts draws on a range of international sources to identify materials of interest to those concerned with special needs education. In 2010, there were 12,274 records in the database.

Exploring issues related to college students in transition may lead the researcher to databases in a variety of academic disciplines. Outside of education, the most likely searches will be in databases for research in sociology and psychology. Databases are also available for theses and dissertations in all academic disciplines. Descriptions of three additional resources are offered below.

CSA Sociological Abstracts draws from the international literature in sociology and related disciplines in the social and behavioral sciences. The database provides abstracts of journal articles and citations to book reviews obtained from more than 1,800 serials publications, as well as abstracts of books, book chapters, dissertations, and conference papers.

PsychINFO is a scholarly index providing citations and abstracts of international journal articles and current chapter and book coverage with monthly updates.

Dissertations and Theses includes more than 2 million entries about doctoral dissertations and master's theses. Dissertations published from 1980 onward include 350-word abstracts written by the author. Master's theses published from 1988 onward include 150-word abstracts. Titles available as native or image PDF formats include free 24-page previews.

Contextual Literature

Researchers begin literature searches on the college student experience with well-known and important current works about the context of higher education that are directly related to their scholarly interests. New researchers commonly make the mistake of defining the context of the topic of interest too broadly, including forces far removed from their topic area. If the study is about learning outcomes achieved by first-year students studying abroad, the contextual literature review need not start with an exhaustive examination of all study abroad experiences over time and across the world. Launching a narrow contextual literature review and working outward as necessary may save the researcher countless hours reading materials that may later prove only peripherally germane to her or his project. A good question to ask when starting the literature review is, Has the exact or similar study to the one I wish to conduct been done by others and, if so, what contextual, substantive, and methodological resources did those researchers use?

Substantive Literature

In addition to reviewing classic and other readings widely considered important in the slice of the higher education context linked to an emerging research problem, a literature search also focuses on substantive writing from authors who have previously or are currently studying the topic. For the first college year, for example, a source often accessed initially for substantive guidance is Upcraft, Gardner, and Barefoot's *Challenging and Supporting the First-Year Student* (2005). Two publications for the study of the first college year available through the National Resource Center—*Guidelines for Evaluating The First-Year Experience at Two-Year Colleges, 2nd Edition* (Gardner, Barefoot, & Swing, 2001a) and *Guidelines for Evaluating The First-Year Experience at Four-Year Colleges, 2nd Edition* (Gardner, Barefoot, & Swing, 2001b)—raise questions for self-study committees and may suggest research questions related to the first year and other aspects of the college student experience. For example, the two-year guidelines ask how the first year has laid a foundation for desired student outcomes and how well the first year at the two-year school has prepared students to transfer to a four-year institution. Among other suggestions, the guidelines for four-year institutions recommend that administrators examine the integration experience of commuter students and how institutional fund raising is linked to programming for first-year students. Researchers interested in studying these or other aspects of the college student experience may pose and answer similar questions.

For the first college year and other student transitions, researchers can proceed to the indices of the *Journal of The First-Year Experience & Students in Transition* (Appendix A) and its predecessors, the *Journal of The Freshman Year Experience* and the *Journal of The Freshman Year Experience & Students in Transition*. This journal contains peer-reviewed articles that describe research results on applied programs for first-year students and other students in transition. For current news on trends in supporting students in transition and ideas on research topics, researchers may also find *E-Source for College Transitions* (Appendix A) useful. This bi-annual newsletter published by the National Resource Center reports on practical strategies for supporting student learning and success and includes assessment outcomes from studies employing both qualitative and quantitative research approaches.

Researchers may also wish to review National Resource Center monographs and reports on first-year seminars, including the *2009 National Survey of First-Year Seminars: Ongoing Efforts to Support Students in Transition* (Padgett & Keup, in press), *2006 National Survey of First-Year Seminars: Continuing Innovations in the Collegiate Curriculum* (Tobolowsky & Associates, 2008); *Exploring the Evidence, Volume III: Reporting Research on First-Year Seminars* (Tobolowsky, Cox, & Wagner, 2005), *Exploring the Evidence: Initiatives in the First College Year* (Troxel & Cutright, 2008), and *The 2003 National Survey of First-Year Seminars: Continuing Innovations in the Collegiate Curriculum* (Tobolowsky, 2005). National Resource Center monographs addressing transition periods beyond the first year include *Shedding Light on Sophomores: An Exploration of the Second College Year* (Tobolowsky & Cox, 2007) and *Graduate Students in Transition: Assisting Students Through the First Year* (Tukuno, 2008). In 2007, The National Resource Center published the fourth edition of *The First-Year Experience in American Higher Education: An Annotated Bibliography* (Koch, Foote, Hinkle, Keup, & Pistilli, 2007). A complete list of print resources, including research reports on first-year students and other students in transition, is available at the Center's website (Appendix A) as are archives of listserv posts on issues related to first-year students, sophomores, seniors, transfer students, assessment, and related topics.

Since the National Resource Center's 30-year-old body of work is primarily focused on student transitions, it is the most likely place to find substantive literature on this topic. However, it is by no means the only place. The researcher should also become familiar with other applicable journals and periodicals, such as *About Campus, Assessment Update, Change, College Teaching, Journal of American Indian College Persistence, Journal of College Student Retention, Journal of Developmental Education, Liberal Education, National On-Campus Report, National Teaching & Learning Forum, Recruitment & Retention in Higher Education, Student Affairs Today, The Hispanic Outlook in Higher Education, The Journal of Blacks in Higher Education, The Journal of College Orientation and Transition, The Journal of College Student Development, The Review of Higher Education,* and *The Teaching Professor.* Several online-only journals are also available and may be accessed by entering appropriate key words into the databases described above.

The substantive literature search can also take the researcher to the recommendations for future research section of previously published studies, which offer ideas for extending current research or exploring new areas. The methodologies that should accompany these new or expanded research questions can be found in these sections.

Finalizing a research question (in quantitative research, a hypothesis) becomes a natural result of the substantive literature review. A few of the hundreds of research questions available for study are offered as examples below. Anyone who reads the literature will come across many more questions that deserve exploration. One question that continues to interest practitioners and researchers is the extent to which faculty development initiatives for those who teach in first-year seminars improves teaching (McClure, Atkinson & Wills, 2008). New teaching techniques may include strategies for encouraging class discussion, using collaborative learning, and offering immediate feedback (Erickson, Peters & Strommer, 2006; Friday, 1989, 1990; Seldin, 1990) or the impact of curricular learning communities on other courses (Smith, MacGregor, Matthews & Gabelnick, 2004). Another research question measures student development during the first year, a question also worthy of consideration at the sophomore and senior years and for transfer students. A life-tasks questionnaire designed by Brower (1990, 1994), for example, allows first-year students to list their most important developmental tasks during the first semester on campus.

Additional research using this measurement instrument or other student development instruments can compare college students across time and/or across groups (Bowman, 2010).

Other research questions prompt investigation into the social and academic integration of students at a variety of transition points (Christie & Dinham, 1991; Krause, 2007; Kuh, Schuh, Whitt, & Associates, 1991; Tinto, 1987; Walpole et al., 2008), the value of summer reading programs (Liljequist & Stone, 2009), the effects of service-learning (Stewart, 2009), the results of intrusive advising (Earl, 1988), and the impact of parental involvement (Harmon & Rhatigan, 1990; Hinni & Eison, 1990; Hofer, 2008). Often, research questions also lead to the exploration of the consequences of programmatic interventions on retention, academic performance, graduation rates, and student satisfaction (Bryson, Smith, & Vineyard, 2002; Starke, Harth, & Sirianni, 2001). More recently, student-learning outcomes in a variety of settings, both curricular and cocurricular, have become a focus of assessment and research efforts (Smith, Goldfine, & Windham, 2009; Tieu & Prancer, 2009). While the substantive literature review may suggest an almost infinite number of possible research studies, each researcher must decide the quality and feasibility of individual questions by discussing them with colleagues before launching a study. This decision is also influenced by time, budget, the researcher's interest, and, in a graduate student's case, the interests and wishes of faculty advisory committee members with whom the student is working.

Methodological Literature

Methodological literature is the third important body of work to examine when preparing to study the college student experience. Hundreds of scholarly books and journal articles are available on the subject of research design, including methods, procedures, and analytical techniques. Years ago, Hoover (1991) offered guidelines for conducting quantitative research on retention of first-year students while *The Freshman Year Experience Newsletter* (Fidler & Hoover, 1991) presented a research design to overcome the problem of volunteers in applied research. Hossler (1991), Ketkar and Bennett (1989), and Iaccino (1989) suggested techniques that can be implemented to evaluate first-year programs. Astin (1991) compared research terminology across several disciplines, reviewed previous findings, and identified questions that, at that time, needed to be studied in higher education. Since the early 1990s, advice on methods for conducting research on the college student experience has proliferated. The following scholarly journals offer valuable guidance on quantitative, qualitative, and mixed methods research and may be accessed using the databases described above: *British Educational Research Journal, Educational Action Research, Educational and Psychological Measurement, Educational Research, Educational Research Quarterly, Educational Researcher, International Journal of Qualitative Studies in Education, International Journal of Research & Method in Education, Issues in Educational Research, Journal of Educational Measurement, Measurement: Interdisciplinary Research and Perspectives, Multivariate Behavioral Research, Review of Educational Research,* and *The Journal of Mixed Methods Research.*

The methodological literature search may also begin with a review and comparison of quantitative and qualitative research methods. A thorough understanding of the purposes, strengths, and weaknesses of both approaches guards against conducting research with a design unsuitable for answering the research question. Early on, most research studies on students in their first college year and other students in transition relied heavily on quantitative designs, including studies using experimental and control groups and studies examining the attitudes and characteristics of entire populations through surveys subjected to statistical analyses. Dependent variables, such as retention and grade point average, and independent variables (e.g., gender, grade level) are highly quantifiable and easily measured and continue to be used to frame quantitative research into the college student experience. In the past two decades, just as many researchers have begun to ask questions best answered using qualitative techniques as described in the chapter 3. The methodology selected depends entirely on the question under study.

To return to the examples offered early in this chapter, a question suited to quantitative design is, What is the correlation between involvement in intensive academic advising and academic success among sophomores? For a qualitative researcher, a more appropriate question would be, How do Latinas experience a science-technology-engineering-math summer bridge program? Researchers using a mixed-method approach (i.e., both quantitative and qualitative), might ask, What is the relationship of scores on a pre-post critical thinking rubric (quantitative data) to self-reported learning (qualitative data) among seniors in an interdisciplinary capstone course? During the literature review, the researcher should take care to note exactly what aspects of a program or components of the student experience previously published researchers suggest for examination and the methodologies used to complete their task.

Conclusion

Educators who work to improve the experience of college students, especially students facing transitional periods, are typically driven by a passion for the work. At their best, these educators combine this passion with a solid understanding of how students experience college, what helps or hinders the students' progress, and what outcomes result from their experience. To provide that information is the important role of the researcher. Her or his task begins with asking a question that matters to practitioners and scholars, understanding what has been said before about that question, and choosing an appropriate approach to answering the question. The preparation phase is arguably the most important component of a research project, and the level of quality with which it is conducted can make or break an entire project. At some point, however, preparation ends and data collection begins. That is the subject of upcoming chapters.

CHAPTER 2
Identifying and Selecting the Methodology

Once a research interest has been identified and honed to a question of focus for study, there are a number of different ways to approach the research process. Subjecting one's intellectual curiosity to the rigor of an empirical study represents a web of decisions that creates the structure for the research process. These decisions are informed by a number of different factors including the topic of study, the context of the research project, ethical concerns, and the available resources. Further, despite efforts to minimize bias in this process, it is impossible to entirely separate the researcher from the study. Therefore, the researcher's background, worldview, learning style, and interests impact the way that she or he approaches the research study as fully as it influences the selection of the topic. The combination of these factors (i.e., topic, context, participants, and researcher) are what make research in the field of higher education, student success, and student transitions so rich and interesting.

The focus of this chapter is on the identification and selection of the research methodology. However, as with other sections of this book, it is critical that we address some important definitional elements as early as possible in this discussion. In particular, what is meant by methodology? In research, the term *methodology* refers to the overarching approach or design for examining phenomenon in higher education. While it may be tempting to use the term *method* as a synonym for methodology, method is, in fact, quite different and refers to the host of approaches and tactics for executing the methodology. In their discussion about ensuring the quality of research, Jones, Torres, and Arminio (2006), help clarify the relationship between methodology and methods. More specifically, they indicate that methodology "is the approach, plan of action, and design" of the research and it "provides the direction for the method," addresses a clear question, and offers clarity on how data are gathered and the means for their interpretation (pp. 123-124). Method has a clear connection with methodology and is "the collection of data" and the procedures for conducting research (p. 180). In short, methodology represents the research strategy, and method represents the tactics to conduct the research.

All social science research draws from two methodological approaches: qualitative inquiry and quantitative procedures. In many instances, these two methodologies are considered to be at odds with one another and are often articulated as two methodological camps. It is the intent of the authors to avoid this approach, which, at best, represents an oversimplification of research methodology and, at worst, advances an adversarial relationship between methodologies and researchers. Instead, this book promotes a positive understanding of each methodology on its own and with respect to the other. Too often in the field, myths and assumptions about each approach are circulated that can diminish higher education research to its own version of warring factions (Figure 2.1). It is hoped that the structure, inclusive approach, and content of this book will highlight the strengths of each methodology, dispel any misunderstandings, and even promote the use of both approaches in combination as a part of mixed-methodology studies.

This chapter begins with a review and comparison of quantitative and qualitative research methods. In an earlier book on this topic, Fidler and Henscheid (2001) aptly stated that "a thorough understanding of the purposes, strengths, and weaknesses of both methodologies guards against conducting research with a design unsuitable for answering the research question" (p. 13). Historically, more research studies in higher education, including research on students in transition, have relied heavily upon quantitative designs. While, on occasion, studies have included experimental conditions and control groups, more often higher education research conducted in the quantitative tradition examines attitudes, characteristics, and outcomes of student populations through data collected by surveys that are subjected

Myths About Qualitative Research	Myths About Quantitative Research
• If you hate statistics, qualitative is for you!	• Quantitative researchers hate people.
• Qualitative methodology is easier than quantitative.	• There is no real thinking involved in quantitative methods; all you have to do is point and click and SPSS does the rest for you.
• All you have to do is talk to people when conducting qualitative research.	
• The shortest distance between fiction and fact is a focus group.	• Numbers geeks who are not comfortable talking to people should do quantitative research.
• Storytelling gets published as research? You've got to be kidding me!	• Quantitative methodology yields factual evidence. (You can't argue with statistics.)
• You can't ever really *know* anything when you do qualitative research.	• You can always manipulate the numbers to get the outcome you want (there are three kinds of lies: lies, damn lies, and statistics).
	• You never know what numbers really mean.

Figure 2.1. Myths about research methodologies.

to statistical analysis. Outcomes of interest[1], such as retention, satisfaction, and academic achievement, as well as characteristics and experiences of the populations under study (e.g., gender, grade level, participation in particular curricular or cocurricular programs)[2] are often highly quantifiable, easily measured, and have been used readily to frame research about the college student experience (Fidler & Henscheid). However, more recently, higher education scholars, practitioners, and decision makers have been calling for a more nuanced approach to capture the complexities of student transition and success. Thus, qualitative inquiry has been used more frequently and received greater acceptance and position in higher education literature. After a discussion of each methodology individually, this chapter addresses the use of both qualitative and quantitative strategies within mixed-methodological studies of the college student experience. A discussion of the points of consideration in making the choice between qualitative and quantitative research designs is offered thereafter.

Qualitative Research

In his book on research design, Creswell (2009) offers a brief but comprehensive definition of qualitative research as

a means for exploring and understanding the meaning individuals or groups ascribe to a social or human problem. The process of research involve[s] emerging questions and procedures; collecting data in the participants' setting; analyzing the data inductively, building from particulars to general themes; and making interpretations of the meaning of data. The final written report has a flexible writing structure. (p. 232)

---

[1] Outcomes of interest are often referred to as dependent variables in quantitative studies and are explained and discussed in chapter 4.

[2] Independent variables are the quantitative means of measuring characteristics of populations of interest in higher education research and are addressed more fully in chapter 4.

Fundamentally, qualitative methodology is about understanding how an individual or group makes meaning of a process or experience. Broadly speaking, the purpose of qualitative research is "to achieve an understanding of how people make sense out of their lives, to delineate the process (rather than the outcome or product) of meaning making, and to describe how people interpret what they experience" (Merriam & Simpson, 2000, p. 97). Given its purpose, it is evident how qualitative inquiry can be a valuable methodology to study the rich and complex array of experiences that students have as they transition into, through, and out of college.

Qualitative research is typically concerned with understanding the individual within a particular context. Given this emphasis on where participants have their experiences and make meaning of their lives, the setting itself becomes a source of data, and qualitative researchers often go to the location of the individuals, groups, or phenomenon under study to collect their data. Such a naturalistic approach to research means that even if data collection is videotaped and analyzed elsewhere, the insight gained from being in the same space as the participant allows the researcher to consider context in the analysis of the data. In this process, the researcher becomes the primary instrument for data collection but also draws data from multiple sources to understand the experiences of individuals and groups in that context (e.g., interviews, observation, document analysis).

Given that qualitative inquiry is conducted in a naturalistic fashion and focused on capturing the essence of human experiences and phenomena, typically, it is not possible to set the parameters of this work a priori. Therefore, qualitative methodology is inductive in nature and builds meaning and theory from the research procedure itself, a process that is often referred to as *bottom up* in its directionality. In other words, "the abstractions are built as the particulars that have been gathered are grouped together" (Bogdan & Biklen, 1998, p. 6). An appropriate analogy is the process of assembling the pieces of a puzzle without seeing the cover of the puzzle box depicting the complete image; the researcher must fit the pieces together and let the picture materialize during the process. Since the ultimate picture is emerging as the data are collected and analyzed without the constriction of being tied to hypothesis testing (or the cover on the puzzle box in this analogy), methods rely upon open-ended questions and processes. Thus, qualitative research is highly interpretive. Further, the goal of this process is to fully understand the unique experience and process of meaning-making for specific individuals and groups in their natural settings rather than trying to learn absolute truths that can be applied in every setting for all individuals. In other words, it is not the intention of qualitative research for findings to be generalized. Instead, these findings lead to the generation and advancement of theory, which can then be applied to similar settings or like populations.

Commonly used methods (i.e., approaches) for collecting data in qualitative methodology include

- Interviews with students either individually or in small groups (typically called a focus group)
- Observations of members of the population of interest in their natural setting
- Analyses of documents or other text-based artifacts generated by the study participants or community where they belong
- Reviews of the literature and meta-analyses of existing research
- Open-ended survey items

A common element of these qualitative methods is that they produce text-based data, whether it is generated by the participants through open-ended survey items and interviews, the researcher (e.g., notes and observations from naturalistic field-work), or other scholars or authors as with literature reviews or document analyses. Qualitative researchers analyze text as data points and strive to organize, focus, and reduce the data into meaningful themes or patterns so that "final conclusions can be drawn and verified" (Miles & Huberman, 1994, p. 11).

Kim (2009) uses qualitative methodology in her study of the role of peer networks in the adjustment process of minority immigrant students during their first year of college. More specifically, she uses data collected via "in-depth, semi-structured, open-ended interviews with individual participants to elicit rich, detailed accounts" (p. 13) of the first-year experiences of 49 immigrant students at a large public university in the Midwest region of the United States. Two research questions guided the study: "(a) What are the academic adaptation experiences of minority immigrant students during their first year in college? and (b) How do peer networks play a role in providing minority immigrant students with support and resources for college adjustment and first-year persistence?" (p. 12). Narrative data collected via one-on-one interviews with participants in this study were analyzed using grounded theory and thematic coding techniques to yield three categories of findings. First, participants had high expectations for their college experience but struggled initially to meet those expectations, specifically with respect to the academic domain of college. Second, immigrant students in this study tended to "primarily rely on friends, family, and relatives over institutional staff for academic support when meeting academic demands" (p. 24). Third, immigrant students relied heavily upon peer networks comprised of students from their same ethnicity during the first year of college, which had a positive impact on participants' academic adjustment and persistence to the second year of college. Overall the selection of a qualitative approach allowed for a deep and nuanced look at the college adjustment experiences of immigrant students and a thorough exploration of the support structures that facilitated their success.

Quantitative Research

While it would be tempting to merely frame quantitative research as a strict converse to qualitative inquiry, that would support the notion that qualitative and quantitative methodologies are at odds with one another when they are, in fact, more complementary in nature. It would also shortchange the unique purposes of each perspective as a research strategy, which are outlined more fully in Figure 2.2. While qualitative methodology is typically used to generate theory, quantitative methodology is a means of testing theories by examining relationships among measurable conditions, also known as variables (Creswell, 2009). The primary purpose of quantitative research is to take steps toward the determination of "the cause of events and to be able to predict similar events in the future" (Merriam & Simpson, 2000, p. 52). The process and reporting of quantitative methodology is typically more formulaic than for qualitative inquiry with more grounded methods and a "final written report...has a set structure consisting of introduction, literature and theory, methods, results, and discussion" (Creswell, p. 233).

Because quantitative methodology seeks to identify potentially causal relationships between variables and to test theory, research conducted in this tradition is highly deductive and product, rather than process, oriented. Quantitative inquiry draws heavily from previous theory and research in

Qualitative Research	Quantitative Research
"The overall purposes of qualitative research are to achieve an understanding of how people make sense out of their lives, to delineate the process (rather than the outcome or product) of meaning-making, and to describe how people interpret what they experience" (Merriam & Simpson, 2000, p. 97).	"It is a means for testing objective theories by examining the relationship among [measurable] variables" (Creswell, 2009, p. 233) and "to be able to predict similar events in the future" (Merriam & Simpson, p. 52).
• Text-based data	• Number-based data
• Researcher is key instrument	• Researcher is detached and enacts use of data collection instrument (e.g., survey)
• Data come from multiple sources (i.e., interviews, observation, document analysis)	• Data usually come from one primary source (e.g., survey instrument, student records data)
• Emergent research design	• Research design crafted prior to data collection
• Less generalizable	• More generalizable
• Research is interpretive	• Data are measurable
• Holistic	• Specific
• Inductive	• Deductive
• Themes, patterns, interpretation	• Statistical interpretation
• Open-ended questions	• Close-ended questions
• Emerging approaches and methods	• Predetermined approaches

Figure 2.2. Comparison of qualitative and quantitative methodology.

an effort to fill gaps in our understanding; test our assumptions; predict behavior and outcomes; and determine the impact of programs, experiences, and intentional interventions. To guide this process, quantitative studies are typically very purposeful with specific testing conditions and measurement tools in mind that are crafted prior to data collection. Further, the intent and outcome for the study are articulated and guided by specific research questions or predictions for the outcome.[3] Drawing again from our puzzle analogy, quantitative methodology seeks to identify the final picture in advance and then determine the conditions under which the construction of the pieces actually creates the desired picture in every scenario.

In order to maintain the focus of the study on the participants and enhance the ability to generalize the findings beyond a single condition, the relationship between researcher and population under study is intended to be distant and detached. This is primarily achieved by using a fully vetted, highly objective instrument for data collection that is selected or developed in advance and that remains unchanged throughout the study. The intent is that minimizing the presence of the researcher in the study will reduce bias in the examination of relationships between the participants and conditions of interest. As such, the findings from quantitative inquiry can, hopefully, be determined to be the result of the conditions under study and, thus, applicable to other situations or environments where those conditions also exist.

Historically, the most common conditions for quantitative data collection have been an experimental design in which a treatment or intervention is tested by randomly assigning participants to receive the treatment or not and controlling for all other factors. While this may be appropriate in medical research, the social sciences, and especially education, rarely allow for the researcher to have such universal controls over a situation or the liberty to randomly assign students to treatment conditions. Given the number of phone calls that college and university staff members receive from concerned parents regarding standard residence hall assignments and classroom grades, one can only imagine the response that a student's denial to a specific curricular or cocurricular program in the interest of research would receive!

---

[3] These predictions for the study are typically expressed as hypotheses in a quantitative study and are addressed more fully in chapter 4.

Therefore, quantitative educational research is much more reliant upon a quasi-experimental condition in which the researcher does not randomly assign students to groups. Instead, a researcher pursuing a quasi-experimental design collects as much data as possible about the participants in order to statistically minimize the impact of nonrandom assignment and to hone in on the relationships of interest between variables during data analysis. To achieve this, a common data collection tool in quantitative methodology for education is the survey instrument, which can collect a large amount of numeric data in evenly measured increments. The data collected by a survey, which is sometimes complemented by student records data (e.g., registrars' data for grades, graduation database for retention), can then be analyzed using a number of different statistical approaches to identify associations between variables, prove or disprove hypotheses, and test theories.

Quantitative methodology was used in Mills' (2010) study of the relationship between participation in a student success course at a community college and student engagement. More specifically, Mills used data from 1,909 students at four community colleges who participated in the Community College Survey of Student Engagement (CCSSE) to address two research questions: (a) "How does participation in an extended orientation student success course influence engagement in college?" and (b) "What assessment capacities are produced by using CCSSEE engagement constructs as outcome measures in success course research?" (p. 11). Multiple quantitative analyses, primarily regression, were used in this study to examine relationships between the variables of interest, namely student success course participation and various measures of student engagement. Results of these analyses indicated "modest but positive course influence on use of support services, faculty interaction, and active and collaborative learning" for the community college students in this study (p. 9). Further, the findings from this quantitative research study provided important evidence regarding structural elements of the course and assessment practices. Notably, there was generally "weak alignment between course goals and engagement outcomes" (p. 9) and "engagement data could make a valuable contribution to assessing current success course practice and developing strategies to improve future outcomes" (p. 27).

Mixed-Methodology

Quantitative and qualitative methodologies are generally unique in approach, assumptions, and strategies. However, when used in combination, these methodologies can yield rich findings, conclusions, and implications to advance our knowledge of undergraduate students in transition. It is now difficult to identify a topic in higher education research that has not generated a body of work that includes studies from both methodological traditions and the use of both methodologies is becoming more frequent within the same study, what is known as mixed-methods research. Further, "with the development and perceived legitimacy of both qualitative and quantitative research in the social and human sciences, mixed-methods research, employing the combination of quantitative and qualitative approaches, has gained in popularity" (Creswell, 2009, p. 203).

Mixed-methodology research draws on the strengths of both qualitative research (e.g., highly descriptive, contextual, generation of theory) and a quantitative approach (e.g., generalizability, potential for the identification of causal relationships, theory testing) and brings them together in the same study. For instance, a researcher can generate a breadth of understanding on an area of research interest from quantitative methodology and yet still explore the depth and complexity of that same issue via qualitative methodology. A mixed-methodology study also can explore and generate the basic tenets of a model or theory (qualitative) and then test and confirm those assumptions (quantitative). Such a study has the potential to offer multiple perspectives on a student issue or experience and, thus, vastly broaden the scope of our understanding of undergraduate education.

Although it is possible to conduct both quantitative and qualitative portions of a mixed-methodology study simultaneously, most commonly done with the use of open-ended items on a survey, it is more typical that one precedes the other and that the second portion of a mixed-methodology study builds upon the first. For example, qualitative procedures may be used first to review the knowledge base on a topic or area of interest and identify gaps in the literature or theory followed by a quantitative approach to address those holes. Qualitative methodology may precede quantitative when a researcher is trying to develop the content of a data collection tool. Focus groups or interviews with students may help a researcher define terms, refine the wording of questions, and establish response options that are meaningful to the target population and, thus, more likely to generate useful information for the research study. Quantitative methodology also is a useful follow-up to qualitative research as a way of testing the conclusions and generalizability of the findings from qualitative inquiry. Conversely, qualitative methodology may follow the collection of data using quantitative means in a research project in order to learn more about the content and complexity of the topic that was studied with a survey or experimental method.

In their study on the transition experiences of students at a Canadian university, Brady and Allingham (2007) provide a wonderful example of mixed-methods research on undergraduate students. They first employed qualitative methods "to generate areas of inquiry that [were] later verified through a quantitative method" (p. 53). More specifically, these researchers conducted an in-depth review of the literature on the topic of high school to college transition models and associated manifestations of student anxiety. The themes and issues identified via that qualitative analysis led to the development of a survey instrument (quantitative) to collect data in order to "confirm or reject the existence of the phenomenon identified earlier in the literature review" (p. 53). Finally, textual data generated via open-ended items (qualitative) included on the survey allowed these researchers to explore the range of transition experiences among study participants and students' reflections upon their preparation for college, as well as have students describe specific sources of stress. Through this mixed-methods study, these researchers found that secondary school preparation was an important, although not uniformly positive, influence on the transition experiences of new college students. Both the results of statistical analyses of survey data and quotes drawn from participants' responses to open-ended items in this study identified that some students who experienced high levels of support in high school felt especially isolated in their first year of college and struggled with the adjustment to reduced levels of support in their postsecondary educational experience (Brady & Allingham).

Selecting a Methodology

While understanding the general characteristics, tactics, and outcomes of quantitative and qualitative methodologies is important to the research process, it also begs the question among new and even experienced researchers: Which methodology is the "right" one to use for the study? In truth, there are a number of issues, which range from mundane to sophisticated, that direct the researcher to a methodology. For the purposes of the discussion in this book, these issues are placed under three major categories that influence the selection of methodology in research: (a) functional elements, (b) the purpose of the study, and (c) the researcher's perspective.

Functional Elements

As much as researchers would like to be able to control all aspects of their study, it is nearly impossible to do so, especially in social science research. Further, studying college students, particularly at points of transition, and capturing the complexity of this important experience in their cognitive, affective, and personal development is an exciting and messy prospect for most researchers. In many ways, it is this messiness that intrigues educational scholars and encourages them to engage in research to help explain the experiences and change among college students. However, it is also important to consider various logistical elements of the research process when selecting a methodology and to acknowledge how those factors can actually direct that decision for the researcher. These include

- *Selection of primary or secondary data analyses.* Regardless of methodology, one of the greatest challenges and investments in the research process is the collection of data. It is always a good step to consider what data currently exist that might address the research question to avoid a costly and difficult step in the research process. While secondary analyses (i.e., analysis of existing data to address research questions for which they were not initially collected) are effective and efficient, they obviously remove the decision about methodology from the researcher directing the current study. For example, hundreds of researchers mine the data collected via national survey instruments, such as the National Survey of Student Engagement (NSSE) and the Cooperative Institutional Research Program's (CIRP) Freshman Survey, to conduct research on the first-year experience via quantitative methodologies. Although less common, researchers should not forget the amount of data already collected via qualitative methodologies, including institutional focus groups and student exit interviews as well as national qualitative studies of student experiences, such the case studies from the Documenting Effective Educational Practice (DEEP) project conducted by the Center for Postsecondary Research at Indiana University (Kuh et al., 2005) or Baxter Magolda's multiple qualitative studies of students' process of self-authorship (summarized in Baxter Magolda, 2009).

- *Audience.* One of the long-held axioms of higher education is that when presenting data, provosts like statistics and presidents like quotes. While not necessarily a firm truth, this statement illustrates the importance of audience in the selection of methodology. In some instances, there are audiences and publication venues that are a better fit for qualitative or quantitative work. Although researchers do not always know all of the segments of higher education that will embrace the findings of their work, at times it is evident that the study at hand will be of particular interest to one audience or another. If that population represents a professional, disciplinary, or philosophical perspective that is more suitable for quantitative or qualitative work, the researcher should use the methodology that will serve as the best communication medium to that audience. For example, if one is researching the experiences of undergraduate students in engineering or economics, quantitative methodology may be more readily accepted by those disciplines. Conversely, qualitative inquiry may be embraced and applied with greater ease by colleagues in the humanities.

- *Timeline.* Although a research agenda can extend throughout a lifetime, there are often significant time considerations for a specific study. Whether it is a window of opportunity for a publication, a deadline to report results for a grant, the need to make progress on a degree, or even access to the population of interest, there are generally some limitations to the duration of a research study. Both quantitative and qualitative methodologies have the potential to be completed quickly or stretched out for several years. However, quantitative inquiry is generally shorter in duration than qualitative research. Outside time constraints need to be considered in the process and may, in fact, dictate the use of one research strategy over the other.

- *Existing research on a topic.* As was discussed in chapter 1 of this volume, research on college students in general, and students in transition in particular, is intimately connected to a body of previous scholarship and empirical work on the topic and to an existing theory base. Original research in the field is intended to fill the gaps in this body of literature. The evolution of a vein of inquiry in higher education often examines an emerging population of interest, introduces new elements of the issue, or tests currently accepted elements of theory. However, many times a significant contribution to the body of work on a topic is to look at the same issue with a new methodological lens. In other words, the decision to conduct a study using one methodology or another is often heavily informed by the existing body of literature on a specific topic.

- *Access to participants.* Obviously, there would be no research without data, and there could be no data without participants in the study. For qualitative work, a researcher must gain access to the environment where the issue under study takes place and the community of interest resides as well as secure the trust of students to participate in the study. Quantitative researchers need to secure approval to disseminate the data collection tool and motivate participants to engage in the experimental condition or complete the survey. Frequently, general access to participants in either methodological scenario is not immediate and is a process fraught with policies, procedures, and gatekeepers (for a more detailed discussion, please see "Principles for Using Human Subjects" on p. 34). While most of these checks are in place to protect the individuals under study in the research and to limit impact upon their environment, there may be significant challenges or limitations to securing access to participants, getting permissions to conduct research, or gaining enough buy-in from participants to collect data. Any or all of these may cause a researcher to abandon a particular research methodology for one that has fewer procedural hurdles with respect to participant access, recruitment, and engagement.

These examples represent only a few of the more functional factors in the research process that affect the selection of one methodology over the other. Although they may feel mundane, their consideration is critical to the selection of the appropriate methodology and the successful outcome of a research study.

Principles for Using Human Subjects

It is important to understand that the study of students in transition falls under the umbrella of social science research and, thus, uses humans as subjects. All human subjects, and especially those from legally protected groups such as legal minors, individuals with developmental limitations, and subjects with limited English skills, are protected by policies, state laws, and federal regulations. These protections are typically grounded in three principles for using human subjects as articulated in the Belmont Report, which was issued by the federal government in 1978 on the topic of medical ethics. These three guiding principles are:

- *Respect*, including protecting the autonomy of all people, treating them with courtesy, and allowing for informed consent to participate in a research study
- *Beneficence*, which represents the balance between maximizing benefits for the research project while minimizing risks to the research subjects
- *Justice*, such that reasonable, nonexploitative, and well-considered procedures are administered fairly

In order to adequately ensure that research on human subjects upholds these principals, most campuses and other research entities have a process by which researchers propose their studies for review by qualified campus personnel and receive approval to conduct the research. These review bodies are called Institutional Review Boards (IRB) and are located on any campus on which medical and human subjects research is allowed. All research involving human subjects, even studies that do not collect original data, are subject to IRB policies and will be discontinued if proper approval procedures are not followed. Researchers should consult with their local IRB to make sure that they are abiding by the necessary principals and policies for human subjects research. Also, researchers should be aware that review processes can take as much as several months and should plan their research timeline accordingly.

Purpose of the Study

In determining which methodology to use, the research question most frequently directs the selection, but this can be a bit baffling. How does the research question drive the methodology? What are the signs that the question is a qualitative or a quantitative one? What happens if a specific research question has not yet been identified? Even experienced researchers can have trouble finding the cues in the research question that suggest one methodology or another.

The true power of a research question to drive the selection of methodology comes from its articulation of the (a) purpose and (b) potential outcomes of the study. The discussion of methodologies both within this chapter and later in this volume provide some suggestions for the type of methodology to use in a research study with respect to the goals and purpose of the study. If the research question is predictive in nature, it is typically a better fit for quantitative methods than if the question is exploratory or interpretive, which lends itself to a qualitative approach (Creswell, 2009; Jones et al., 2006; Merriam & Simpson, 2000). For example, if a researcher is trying to determine causal relationships between participation in a first-year seminar and the rate at which students return for their second year of college, it is more likely that he or she will draw from the quantitative tradition to collect information on students' participation in a first-year seminar, a host of experiences associated with their learning and development in that course, and a reliable measure of first-to-second-year persistence for that population of students and then subject these measures to statistical analyses to identify explanatory relationships between those different variables. However, if a researcher is more interested in the different ways that students in a first-year seminar perceive that their institution provides a supportive climate for new students, it is likely that a qualitative methodology is best to collect students' views of their personal experiences in their own words and observe the environmental cues expressed in those narratives to describe supportive practices. As such, the purpose of the study—seeking empirical evidence or proof as opposed to describing the complexity of phenomenon—is the first tool to use in determining the appropriate methodology.

The most valuable element to help determine the purpose and methodology of the study is the verb used in the research question or, if a solid research question is still evolving, in the discussion of the topic of interest for the study.

The verb will generally identify the purpose, scope, and focus of the study, which then suggests a methodology. For example, *predict* and *explain* suggest the deductive nature of quantitative research while *describe* and *discover* are more suggestive of an inductive character of qualitative work. Figure 2.3 shows a Venn diagram in which qualitative and quantitative methodologies are represented by circles and their overlap represents commonalities between both methodologies or a mixed-methodological approach. In each segment of this diagram, the verbs from research questions and purpose statements of studies published in the *Journal of The First-Year Experience & Students in Transition* are categorized by their frequency of use in quantitative or qualitative studies. With this tool, it is, in fact, feasible to let the question, or at least its verb, drive the methodology in a research project.

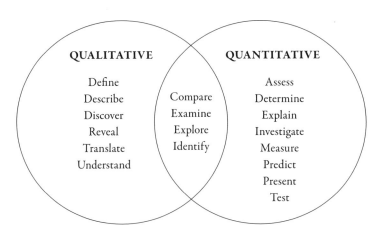

Figure 2.3. Methodological categories for verbs used in research questions on student transitions.

Perspective of the Researcher

As discussed, external issues, most notably the functional elements and purpose of the study, help dictate the selection of methodology. However, it is critical to also consider the perspective, worldview, and strengths of the researcher. While most topics in higher education have the potential to be addressed using qualitative, quantitative, or mixed-methodological approaches, researchers have tendencies in the way that they perceive higher education issues and ideas as well as a common perspective in their approach to examining it. Further, certain types of analytical, writing, and even interpersonal skills lend themselves to either quantitative or qualitative methodologies.

Quantitative research usually draws from a positivist or post-positivist worldview, which assumes that there is an objective, independent reality; that "data, evidence, and rational considerations shape knowledge" (Creswell, 2009, p. 7); and that objectivity is an essential component of high-quality inquiry. Given this foundation, it is perhaps not surprising that individuals who enjoy highly structured work and have a facility with math and statistics are drawn to this methodological perspective. To people who innately see the world through quantitative-colored glasses, complex issues almost naturally break down into measurable parts that can be fit together to create a big picture. As such, they also tend to have strong technical communication skills, particularly with respect to scientific writing and the dissemination of numeric data. While there is an unfavorable stereotype of quantitative researchers as socially awkward, those drawn to this methodology may, in fact, share a preference to work with the calculable expression of people's experiences, as mediated through a survey instrument or a measurement rubric, rather than directly with the participants themselves.

On the other hand, qualitative methods are far more constructivist in their worldview and assumptions. In this philosophy, inquiry is not undertaken for the pursuit of a general understanding of truth or reality, but rather to understand situational, subjective, or localized perceptions of a situation. In other words, reality is socially constructed and truth is subjective (Creswell, 2009, Jones, 2002; Jones et al., 2006). In order to conduct research in line with this philosophy, it is critical that the design, data collection procedures, and data analysis be as flexible as possible to allow for the infinite number of options that can emerge from the research process, most notably through the collection of narrative as opposed to numeric data. Given this reliance upon text and language, individuals who are drawn to qualitative methods tend to enjoy interacting with people, as well as have a great deal of empathy, excellent listening skills, and a greater facility with literary writing. Lest qualitative researchers are cast in an entirely nonscientific fashion, it is important to understand that analytical skills are critical to the success of all researchers, and the qualitative investigator generally uses these skills to organize themes rather than run statistical machinations. Individuals drawn to qualitative research would have the tendency to collect and assemble puzzle pieces but may not have any intention of them fitting together in one picture. In fact, their focus would tend toward understanding the shape of each piece rather than striving to see the assembled whole.

While it is rare that one person sees everything entirely from a quantitative worldview and another only qualitatively, people do have strengths and tendencies that often make one methodology more appealing than the other. Someone with many of the characteristics presented in the quantitative paragraph above will very likely view even the same situation differently than an individual who is more akin to the persona described in the qualitative paragraph. As such, different researchers are likely to see various research possibilities, describe them with different verbs, and pursue their line of inquiry distinctively and, thus, tend toward one methodology or the other.

Conclusion

This chapter has introduced the concept of methodology and its role in the development and execution of high-quality research on the undergraduate student experience. The definitions and summaries of qualitative, quantitative, and mixed methodologies provided in this chapter help create a common foundation and language for readers to continue their development as researchers and to engage in the presentation of research strategies covered in this book. Subsequent chapters will continue to explore methodology (i.e., the overarching approach or design for examining phenomenon in higher education) from the specific perspective of qualitative approaches in chapter 3 and quantitative research in chapter 4. Further, each chapter will build upon the foundation of methodology introduced in this chapter and explore the various approaches and tactics for executing the methodology in a research study (i.e., methods). However, it is important to understand that the ability to identify, select, and discuss methodology as outlined in this chapter goes far beyond any one study, project, or specific chapter of a text. Such knowledge allows higher education professionals to fully engage as both consumers of and contributors to the scholarly dialogue in education and on the topic of college student transition.

CHAPTER 3
Conducting Qualitative Research on College Student Transitions

The essential function of a qualitative study is to describe an individual or group from the participants' own viewpoint by use of research techniques such as field observations, focus groups, unstructured interviews, limited surveys, and document analysis. Researchers will generally choose a qualitative approach when they wish to determine how an individual or group understands or makes meaning of a process, be it an event, activity, program, or period of time. It is the actions of individuals and groups in their natural or day-to-day context that drive qualitative research, and the theory, theme, or thesis of the study emerges during data collection and analysis. Qualitative studies are, thus, referred to as naturalistic inquiry and as having an emergent design that is guided by a general question, not an a priori hypothesis. The qualitative researcher studying college students in transition does not attempt to describe or understand external influences, such as the effect of a Supplemental Instruction program or the environment of a classroom or residence hall, from outside the viewpoint of the participants.

For example, studies of tribal colleges where effectiveness measures such as retention and grade point average may not be the most important success factors to students or faculty members would include observations and interviews that illuminate the goals that are of value to members of this kind of campus community. One key advantage of qualitative research is its role in making sense of a situation in need of in-depth explanation. Qualitative studies on student transitions are a good way, for example, to understand the meaning sophomores make of their actions as they move between academic majors, to clarify professors' beliefs about the role first-year seminar instructional development plays in the evolution of their teaching practices, and to reveal what happens in a service-oriented senior capstone course.

Along with describing in rich detail what is happening in a particular setting, qualitative research can be used for theory generation about a particular social phenomenon. One may, with some caution, generalize the theory to similar settings. A qualitative study may also be used to confirm or contest the efficacy of extant theories. For example, in her study of first-year international students, Andrade (2005) confirmed the usefulness of applying some aspects of traditional persistence theories, such as the importance of involvement and integration to international students. In another study, patterns of engagement among students who transfer between four-year institutions were studied by Kirk-Kuwaye and Kirk-Kuwaye (2007) to reveal that these students have as many difficulties becoming involved in their transfer institutions as students moving from two-year to four-year institutions. Whatever the specific purposes of their studies, qualitative researchers studying students in transition are all committed to gaining and sharing broad, holistic insights into actions and viewpoints of individuals and groups in settings relevant to those transitions. They do this from the belief that such research is intrinsically valuable and that developing insights into specific settings and/or populations can help us better our understanding of the phenomenon under investigation.

The purpose of this chapter is to explicate the process researchers use to conduct qualitative studies, beginning with a description of the role and common dispositional characteristics of the qualitative researcher. The chapter then turns to a discussion of the process for crafting the research proposal, selecting approaches to conducting a study, choosing data collection procedures, and selecting types of data to collect. These sections are followed by descriptions of data analysis, trustworthiness, as well as writing up the report. The chapter concludes with a few final thoughts about using a qualitative research approach to better understand students in transition.

The Role and Disposition of the Qualitative Researcher

Fundamental to qualitative research is the concept of researcher as instrument, which holds that observers of social phenomenon, even those committed to following strict research conventions (both quantitative and qualitative), bring personal biases to the observation. These biases must be acknowledged and bracketed (i.e., taken into account as the study is designed and data collection and analysis proceed). Qualitative researchers do not use Geiger counters, spectrometers, or microscopes to test phenomena; they use themselves, which means that candid self-awareness is a critical dispositional trait one brings to this kind of scholarly activity. Along with self-awareness, successful qualitative researchers share several other characteristics, including

- *Strong writing abilities.* Qualitative data are reported in narrative, with the qualitative case being built through rich description of the research setting and the actions and viewpoints of individuals and groups arising from that setting. High-quality writing is at the center of the qualitative research project.
- *Empathy and excellent listening skills.* The qualitative researcher's task is to subordinate her or his own viewpoint and to deeply understand that of the individuals participating in the study. Successful qualitative researchers bring their full attention to bear on the words and actions of others. They attempt to listen without judgment to what is said (and left unsaid) by study participants.
- *Patience.* Qualitative researchers build relationships with their study's participants, whether those participants are human beings, photographs, or 100-year-old diaries. This relationship building takes considerable time and a willingness to allow meaning to emerge rather than be forced out of the data. One product of impatience in qualitative research is a report with an obvious mismatch between data and analysis.
- *Organizational skills.* The data collected by a qualitative researcher can be mountainous. Participant observers collect field notes and artifacts from the research site, which may include internal communiqués, photographs, advertising flyers, and handwritten notes. Interviewers and focus group facilitators typically collect audio and written transcripts. Survey administrators accumulate quantitative and qualitative respondent data. Document analysis and literature reviews require amassing boxes of

binders, books, or electronic files. Analysis of any of these data demands organizing, managing, and knowing the contents of what is collected very well. The qualitative researcher either has a natural penchant for organization or acquires those skills.

- *Analytical abilities.* The volumes of data collected during a qualitative research project are subject to ongoing scrutiny by the researcher looking for patterns of meaning. As Miles and Huberman (1994) suggest, analysis is a process of data reduction, data display, conclusion drawing, and verification. These processes draw on the researcher's ability to separate objects or words into their constituent parts, examine them, and reorder them. To the untrained eye, qualitative data can appear to be an unrelated jumble. To the analytical mind, they harbor a well-ordered, sociologically important story.

- *Flexibility.* At the beginning of each semester of a graduate introduction to qualitative research course, a faculty member, who had taught the course for several years, asked students to characterize how comfortable they were with ambiguity—a hallmark of qualitative research. One student, who struggled throughout the course, reported that he was "57.5 % comfortable with uncertainty." Later a fine quantitative researcher, this student could not get used to having questions that originally drove his research project scuttled, or watching one line of inquiry dead-end as five others opened, or recognizing that his exhaustive literature review on a topic suggested by initial data collection would never see publication as subsequent data collection revealed another story. He, and others who venture into qualitative research, must accept the many rabbit holes of this type of research and commit to intellectual flexibility.

Where to Begin—The Research Proposal

Planning is the first critical phase of a qualitative research project and can be facilitated by creating a research proposal concurrent with other preparation done as described in the previous chapters. The proposal written for qualitative research is typically shorter than that composed for a quantitative study and leaves room for the researcher to shift (sometimes dramatically) the focus of data collection as new answers surface to the key question, What is going on here? The emergent nature of qualitative research gives rise to some debate about how structured and comprehensive the research proposal should be. Individual researchers should allow the needs of their research topic and the conventions of their own research communities (e.g., granting or accrediting agencies, dissertation committees, campus administrations, academic departments) to dictate the length and content of the research proposal. Although methodological texts and other guides will employ a variety of terms to describe the sections of a qualitative research proposal, the typical components of this document are described below. Further discussion of several of these components will follow this section.

The Problem of the Study

What prompts this study and what do researchers and/or practitioners not know that would be revealed by conducting this study? This section would include a review of the contextual and substantive literature that supports a need for this study. As noted earlier, both qualitative and quantitative researchers begin their literature review by asking and answering the questions, Has this exact study been conducted by others, and have studies like this been conducted by investigators in education or related fields?

The Purpose of the Study

What specific issue is intended to be the subject of this research? For our purposes, what aspect of college students in transition will be examined? In this section, the research question is presented. The research approach underpinning the study, as discussed in greater detail below, is described here and establishes the exact language that will be used in the wording of the research question and throughout the study.

Research Design and Methodology

This section of the research proposal builds the case for the use of a particular qualitative design and for the specific data collection methods to be employed. At this point, the researcher must make a convincing link between the purpose of the study and the design and demonstrate the logic behind this choice. As described in chapter 2, different research questions warrant different research designs. The research design and methodology section will also enumerate research procedures, which are the chronological outline of each phase of the study, and they will justify the decision to employ each procedure. An in-depth discussion of qualitative design considerations may be found in Denzin and Lincoln (2005); LeCompte, Millroy, and Preissle (1992); Strauss (1987); Strauss and Corbin (1998); and Wolcott (1995). At the proposal stage, the researcher will also design protocols for any interviews or focus groups to be conducted as part of the study. The research design and methodology section, or the proposal appendices, will include these protocols.

Site and Participant Selection

The research proposal next builds a case that the site and participants selected are appropriate for gathering data to answer the research question. Three principles underlie the task of selecting a site and participants for qualitative study. First, is the willingness to build a close relationship with research participants. A qualitative approach necessitates that the researcher spend enough time in the field to collect sufficient data to answer the research question(s). This immersion dictates an often longer-term relationship with the research subjects than is typically experienced in quantitative research. To denote this special relationship in qualitative research, subjects are referred to as participants. Qualitative researchers must take special care in interacting with participants, collecting data, entering, being in, and leaving the site, and in reporting out their findings. The site and participants should be selected with this special relationship in mind.

The second principle involves the theoretical and practical considerations of site and participant selection. The research question, built on the research approach, is the theoretical guide for site and participant selection. Theoretical contrasts (i.e., selecting places and individuals predicted to be on one extreme or the other of the research question) are one helpful method for site and participant selection. For example, participants in a case study of a Supplemental Instruction group could be one individual who by academic background, demographic, or personal characteristics is most likely to fail the course linked to the group's activities and another who would be most likely to succeed. If a comparative study is to be conducted of two or more sites, using these same theoretically contrasting criteria is appropriate. Practical considerations include the researcher's level of access to the site and participants and the amount of time, money, and energy the researcher has to complete the study.

The third principle of site and participant selection is built on a fundamental assumption of qualitative research, as described earlier, that understanding the actions of a small number of individuals holds intrinsic value and/or can lead to an understanding of the actions of a much larger group with similar characteristics. Qualitative researchers do not seek a large representative sample; they seek to study a few individuals whose actions in a particular setting are of value and may predict (or build a theory for) the actions of similar individuals in similar settings.

Ethical Considerations

The research proposal also addresses steps taken to ensure the study is conducted in an ethical manner. Early on, social scientists, including qualitative researchers, adopted ethical guidelines used in medicine (e.g., subjects participate in a study voluntarily and steps must be taken to guard their safety). Qualitative researchers have expanded those guidelines to ensure, in most cases, the anonymity of their participants, to respectfully treat participants as their teachers during data collection, to gain and abide by the participant's written consent in every aspect of the study, and to report the findings of the study truthfully. While qualitative data collection can be engaging, ethical researchers also do not collect data they do not intend to analyze and report. Whether overtly (as is the case for critical theorists, constructivist, and participatory or collaborative researchers) or implicitly (in the case of positivist and postpositivist-guided research), ethical qualitative researchers intend their efforts to have a positive impact on the participants and on the consumers of their research.

Analytical Procedures

The research proposal should include a description of the procedures to be used to analyze the data collected, including procedures for coding the data and how these procedures emerge from the research approach. As noted above, data analysis, including data reduction, data display, conclusion drawing, and verification, will occur throughout data collection. This recursion should be noted in the proposal. At this stage, any qualitative data analysis software intended for use, such as NVivo or Atlas.ti, should also be described and its use justified.

Limitations

Any threats to the generalizability of a study should be described and steps to eliminate them or ameliorate their effects need to be outlined. Limitations fall under several categories, including the nature of the site, the participants, and the researcher. The most effective method for decreasing limitations is to study what *can* be studied. If the research interest is the differential impacts of first-year seminars as it was for Friedman and Marsh (2009), and there is access to two types of seminars, then the researcher's job is to design a study around just those two types of seminars and to make no claims that the study is about all types of seminars. If the investigator has interest in and access to three types of seminars as Rice (1992) did, the research on differential impacts can be about the three. The best qualitative studies offer a tight fit across the research question, the site, the participants selected, and the researcher themselves.

Implications for Future Research and Practice

As the study is conducted, a qualitative researcher typically delimits its scope or, from the beginning, formulates a research question that leaves out as much or more than it leaves in. Once the study is completed, the research findings may lead to questions answerable through further qualitative inquiry or follow-up quantitative studies. These implications for future research are preliminarily described in the research proposal and more exhaustively in the final report. The study may also make new or unique uses of qualitative methodologies, and the researcher may recommend these approaches for replication in future studies. Particularly in critical theory, constructivist, and participatory or collaborative research on students in transition (as described in greater detail in the following section), the impact of the study and its findings on educational practice should be noted.

Outline of the Manuscript

A description of the sections of the research report should be provided in the proposal, as well as a timeline for conducting the study, a budget if costs will be accrued, and strategies for disseminating the results. These dissemination strategies should include submission to peer-reviewed journals and, if appropriate, distribution of findings to internal audiences. As with manuscripts of quantitative research reports on college student transitions, the sixth edition of the *Publication Manual of the American Psychological Association* (2009) is the standard for qualitative research reports on this topic.

Research Approaches

As part of the planning and proposal-writing process, a qualitative researcher establishes and communicates the approach or assumptions about human actions and ways of knowing he or she brings to formulation of the research question, data collection, and data analysis. Five such approaches have been identified by Guba and Lincoln (2005) ranging from positivism to the participatory or collaborative worldview initially forwarded by Heron and Reason (1997). Even as qualitative researchers are open to allowing meaning to emerge from the data they collect, they still carry these fundamental understandings with them into the field. Positivism, the approach adopted by early qualitative researchers, is most closely aligned with the work of quantitative researchers and is often referred to as the scientific method. It holds that a reality exists independent from and unaffected by the actions or beliefs of the individual or group, that this reality transcends history and nationalities and that this reality can be fully discovered through observation and experimentation. By World War II, social scientists had largely abandoned this worldview for a postpositivist approach that suggests that human beings can only know what is real in the world imperfectly and probabilistically. Under postpositivism, there is still a reality outside the individual, but researchers can only conjecture that their findings about sociological action accurately represent this reality. Within the third approach identified by Guba and Lincoln, critical theorists argue that contexts and values (i.e., social, political, cultural, economic, ethnic, and gender) shape what individuals and groups believe is real, reality is a social construct and the focus of study should be both on the knower and on what is known. The value of sociological research, according to critical theorists, lies in its ability to help individuals and groups understand and emancipate themselves from dominant contexts and values. The fourth approach, constructivism, suggests that what individuals and groups perceive to be real is highly localized, subjective, and situational and that the sociological task is to understand—and overcome—constraints on actions inside a locally constructed reality. Finally, theorists who adhere to the participatory or collaborative approach suggest that reality is both cocreated and real. They are primarily interested in how an individual or group uses language in a shared context, how they can know something as a matter of practicality, and how individuals and groups function and thrive by balancing autonomy with cooperation.

In the context of studying college students in transition, a positivist and postpositivist would see their role as providing observable data and analysis to academic administrators and other policy makers who would decide for themselves the implications of the research. A critical theorist would employ similar research methods as those used by positivists and postpositivists but see his or her additional role as an advocate for social transformation. Constructivist researchers are full participants in the actions of their research sites, making no claim that they are separate from the highly localized reality cocreated by study participants. Action research (in which the researcher assumes a partnership with participants to conduct the study and to use its results to address issues of importance to both) is typical of the constructivist paradigm. And, finally, researchers interested in student transitions who adopt the participatory or collaborative approach see themselves as interpreters of the practical day-to-day actions of students, educators, or other stakeholders. They cocreate findings by their presence and also may choose action research methodologies.

The approach under which a researcher operates impacts every aspect of the study, including the research questions asked and the language used to describe participant actions and viewpoints. For example, those who adopt the stance that reality is not a social construction but has fixed properties are interested in the participants' perceptions of that universal reality (outsiders looking in), while researchers who assume the position that reality is a social construction are interested in the participants' perspective (insiders cocreating that reality). Final research reports also strictly adhere to language use that is dictated by the research approach selected. In this chapter, qualitative data collection and analytical methods used across research approaches will be addressed. A finer grained treatment may be found in Guba and Lincoln (2005), Johnson and Christensen (2008), and Wolcott (1995).

Data Collection Procedures and Types of Data

Across all research approaches, standard sources of qualitative data include observations, interviews, focus groups, limited surveys, document analyses, and literature reviews. Some qualitative research questions on issues related to students in transition can lead to the use of several data collection methods in one study. For example, Tinto and Goodsell's (1994) case study of freshman interest groups at the University of Washington used data from document collection and analysis; interviews with students, educators, and administrators; observation; and other qualitative techniques. The researchers sought to understand both the actions and viewpoints of all program participants, necessitating data collection from multiple sources. Similar to Moffatt's *Coming of Age in New Jersey* (1989) and Nathan's *My Freshman Year: What a Professor Learned by Becoming a Student* (2005), Henscheid's (1996) dissertation research was a year-long ethnography into the student perspective of first-year residential learning communities. The latter research involved participant observation in the residence halls and classrooms, interviews, focus groups, limited surveys, photography, and document analysis. Research questions about perspective (e.g., those asked in these studies) demand data collection about the setting, how study participants act in that setting, what they say about how they act, and the consequences of their actions. Whereas Tinto and Goodsell were interested in the perspectives of students, educators, and administrators, Moffatt, Nathan, and Henscheid's research questions focused only on those of the students. Whose perspective is of interest further refines data collection.

If a researcher seeks to answer a question about the actions and viewpoints of participants in one setting, she or he will choose to conduct a single-site case study. If the research question involves contrasting actions and viewpoints across multiple locations or situations a multisite case study is conducted. Data collection methods are standard across both types, with the same forms of data collected at each site of a multisite case study.

Observations

Naturalistic (as opposed to laboratory) observations are a powerful qualitative data collection method because they allow the researcher to answer questions about the actual actions of a participant as they may contrast with the actions the participant self-reports during interviews. Qualitative researchers often begin with the observational portion of a study before moving on to other data collection procedures. For example, Magolda (1997) followed participant observation with in-depth unstructured interviews and document review to examine the actions and beliefs of residential college members. Roderick and Carusetta (2006) used participant observation in the classroom at Renaissance College at the University of New Brunswick and then one-on-one interviews to provide insight into the experiences of first-year students in a problem-based learning context. Along with highlighting incongruities between real and self-reported actions, observations can provide a shared context for the researcher and participant to discuss later, during open-ended interviews.

In qualitative research on student transitions, the observer gains access to the site from an authority responsible for it (e.g., a faculty member or administrator) and typically enters the field (i.e., classroom, residence hall, or organizational meeting) as unobtrusively as possible. How much an observer participates in actions in the field is determined by the research approach adopted for the study and can range from complete noninterference to total immersion. The first few days of observation, when the researcher is typically least familiar with what is happening at the site, are the most critical for recording field notes and for writing researcher memos speculating on the meaning behind the participants' actions. With the research question and unobtrusiveness to guide their actions, observers record field notes in notebooks, on laptop computers, with audio and/or video recording devices or, least obtrusive of all, after the observation session has ended. The length of time the researcher spends in the field, on any single day or over the course of the study, is dictated by the research question. For example, a study of changing student perspectives from the first to the last day of an academic term requires a longer observation period than studying the interactions of students involved in a week-long alternative service break. Exiting the observation field should be done thoughtfully and unobtrusively, and research participants should be thanked and reminded of the study's purpose and of plans for securing the data.

Analysis in the Field

As noted by other authors on qualitative research (e.g., Hammersley & Atkinson, 1983; Maxwell, 1996), this type of scholarly work is recursive, not linear or sequential. Qualitative designs often, and some would argue should always, include a collection of small amounts of preliminary data guided by a broad research question followed by an analysis of data and refinement, narrowing, or complete abandonment of the original question prior to resumption of concurrent data collection and analysis. This recursive nature of qualitative research dictates that data analysis begins almost immediately upon onset of data collection. Evolving data codes, described in greater detail below, therefore become an important component of field notes gathered during observations and interviews and from other sources. Data analysis notations are located in the researcher memos in field notes mentioned above and in separate documents dedicated to detailing the analysis process.

Interviews

Qualitative researchers interested in the meaning research participants make in a social context will conduct interviews that fall along a continuum from highly unstructured, employing a few broad questions, to very structured, involving use of a strict interview protocol and/or narrow questions. Interviews may be coupled with other data collection techniques, such as administration of a limited survey, and are intended to provide participants an opportunity to offer a wide range of responses and the researcher the chance to ask broad questions as well as pointed, follow-up and clarifying questions. The research question drives the choice to conduct interviews, and researchers may use different types of interviews at different points in a study. For example, Fidler, Neururer-Rotholz, and Richardson's (1999) interest in the impact of training on teaching techniques prompted them to follow administration of a close-ended survey to all faculty training participants who taught a first-year seminar with open-ended follow-up interviews with 20 of the participants. The interviews were conducted, in part, to determine what specifically about the training had impacted the participants' teaching approaches. Both closed and open-ended interviews were used by Harmon (2006) to study peer mentors who worked with undergraduate first-year students in learning communities. This researcher's interest was in the students' perceptions of what they learned from their experiences as well as how that learning impacted their personal and professional development.

Open-ended interviews are used at the early stages of a qualitative research project like Harmon's to allow the perceptions of the participants to fully dictate the story as it first emerges. More close-ended follow-up questions allow the researcher to focus in on the data most salient to answering the research question. If, for example, a first-year student who fails to return for a second year of college does not mention an academic advisor when asked about people important in their college experience, the researcher may choose to ask a follow-up question specifically about that omission. The open-ended nature of the first interview allows for an important story about advising to emerge that could not have if the researcher had used a close-ended question.

The research question and practical considerations also drive the methods used for gathering interview data, which may include audio and/or video recording of the interview, face-to-face sessions with the interviewer either writing into a notebook or immediately transcribing the data onto a computer, e-mail exchanges, or uses of online social networking or electronic meeting spaces.

Focus Groups

Group interviews, or focus groups, are conducted when the qualitative researcher is interested not only in individual points of view but in their evolution as they are shared in and shaped by a group interview setting. Focus groups are as much about understanding the norms and processes of a group as they are about collecting data on individual meaning making. The rationale and methods for conducting focus groups are described in greater detail by Bloor, Frankland, Thomas, and Robson in *Focus Groups in Social Research* (2001) and Morgan in *Focus Groups as Qualitative Research* (1997).

Focus groups have practical advantages when a wide variety of data collection methods are in use. For example, in their study of a transition program for first-year students at the University of Kansas, Wolf-Wendel, Tuttle, and Keller-Wolff (1999) paired focus group data with a review of grade point averages, retention rates, and measures of self-efficacy. In another study, Krause (2007) conducted focus group interviews with 46 individuals to explore the nature of undergraduate commuter students' social involvement with peers during the transitional first six months of their university experience. Blackhurst, Akey, and Bobilya (2003) interviewed students in focus groups to explore the outcomes of learning community membership from the participants' points of view and to determine the connections between participants' reported perceptions and behaviors and the measurable outcomes of the program. Focus groups are typically composed of 6 to 12 participants selected for their ability to help the researcher answer the research question and, in general, are homogenous to avoid conflict or clique formation during the focus group interview—unless this tension is of interest to the researcher. Data gathering from more than one focus group is advisable and the use of two moderators—one to pose questions and one for note-taking—is common. A number of roles may be assumed by the primary moderator, as suggested by Krueger (1998) including the seeker of wisdom, the enlightened novice, the expert consultant, the challenger, the referee, the writer, the team member, the therapist, and the serial interviewer. Methods for collecting data from focus groups are similar to those used for one-on-one interviews and are driven by the research question and by practicality.

Limited Surveys

Questionnaires, or limited surveys, are administered in qualitative research to gather demographic, baseline, exploratory, and/or confirmatory data from the study's participants and may precede or follow other forms of data collection. Surveys play a much different role in qualitative research than they do in quantitative research as will be described in chapter 4. Qualitative researchers do not conduct tests of statistical significance on numerical survey data, although their analysis may include frequency counts of responses and some display of descriptive statistics. For example, self-report survey data were used by Windschitl and Leshem-Ackerman (1997) along with frequency counts on e-mail usage of students in three learning groups to discern the relationship between frequency of e-mail use and membership status. In another study (Benjamin, 1993), qualitative and quantitative survey data on 166 Native American students were collected for six years beginning in the students' first year of college. Two survey-based studies were conducted by Milville and Sedlacek (1994) and Noledon and Sedlacek (1996) to gauge student attitudes and self-reported behaviors. The former study focused on attitudes toward Arab American students while the latter explored the attitudes and behaviors of honors students. A cogent description of the role limited surveys and questionnaires may play in qualitative research is offered by Grant and Fine (1992), who also provide other examples of studies that have successfully used these methods.

Document Analysis and Literature Review

Thus far, our discussion has focused on data collection methods that involve human beings as study participants. Substantial understanding of issues related to students in transition has also come from collection and analysis of documents (either alone or in concert with other data collection methods) and from reviews of extant literature. The most recent comprehensive review of literature on the impacts of college on students (Pascarella & Terenzini, 2005) can be considered a literature review in the qualitative tradition. These researchers conducted the same kind of data collection and analysis any qualitative researcher would undertake, on a large scale, to write their meta-analysis of three decades of research into the effects of college. Document reviews (also known as textual analysis) can be performed on policy manuals, student assignments and reflective writing, textbooks, curriculum guides, online discussions in course management systems and social networks, and any other material considered relevant to answering the research question.

The *Journal of The First-Year Experience & Students in Transition* has, over the years, published a number of document and literature reviews on various topics related to students in transition. With an analysis of literature on the college student experience published in 1997, Brower built a stage theory of student decision making during the transition to college. Using a text analysis of transcripts from simulated negotiations at Camp David, Fratrantuono and Senecal (1996) revealed teaching objectives and activities related to those objectives. The authors suggested that this type of text analysis offers a method for discovering both cognitive and affective aspects of the teaching and learning process. In another analysis of literature on the student out-of-class experience and its impact on academic, intellectual, and/or cognitive learning outcomes, Terenzini, Pascarella, and Blimling (1996) drew several conclusions on the interaction effect between out-of-class experiences and these outcomes. Also in 1996, Chaskes used his review of literature on student development theory and immigration patterns to build a theory of the first-year experience as a process of socialization to a new cultural environment similar to that undergone by immigrants. And finally, Gordon (1991) traced the history of a 70-year-old first-year seminar program at Ohio State University through institutional documents to reveal the changing values, context, and character of the program, and to chronicle the program's establishment and maintenance.

Data Analysis

Data analysis is the "explicit, systematic" method used to draw conclusions about data and to carefully test those conclusions. These methods are "credible, dependable, and replicable" (Miles & Huberman, 1994, p. 2) and, according to these authors, include data reduction, data display, and conclusion drawing and verification. As noted earlier, qualitative data collection and analysis are typically conducted simultaneously and recursively. During data reduction, the researcher selects, focuses, simplifies, abstracts, and transforms the data by writing summaries and memos, assigning codes to the data, positing themes, and creating clusters of like data. "Data reduction is a form of analysis that sharpens, sorts, focuses, discards, and organizes data in such a way that 'final' conclusions can be drawn and verified" (Miles & Huberman, p. 11). Reduced data are then displayed using matrices, graphs, charts, maps, networks, and other graphical devices to organize, compress, and assemble information for purposes of drawing conclusions. Graphic representations are helpful for displaying and building an understanding of the relationships between and across activities, people, perspectives, and other qualitative data. Taxonomies and networks are also useful for better understanding social phenomenon. Miles and Huberman's qualitative data analysis sourcebook is especially beneficial here.

Throughout the analysis process, qualitative researchers are drawing and verifying preliminary conclusions about what the data mean until that meaning has passed a final test of confirmability, either through verification by colleagues (i.e., intersubjective consensus or inter-rater reliability) or through efforts to replicate the findings in another data set. The constant comparative method of data analysis (Glaser, 1978) is one example of the recursive process of data gathering, reduction, display, conclusion drawing, and verification.

This analytical method, typically used for building a theory from qualitative data, includes the following steps:

1. Initial data collection
2. Identification of key issues, recurrent events, or activities that may become categories
3. Collection of additional data that provide instances of those categories while remaining conscious of diversity within the categories
4. Descriptions of categories that account for what is seen and continue to look for new instances
5. Ongoing work with data and the emerging model to discover fundamental social processes and relationships
6. Use of purposeful sampling (i.e., seeking out instances that aid in expanding the developing theory), coding, and writing to analyze the primary categories

Whether the research purpose is generation of theory or not, data analysis must account for both those instances that confirm the emerging understanding of the social phenomenon under study and those that do not. Robinson (1951) offered a modified analytic induction procedure that is a helpful companion to the constant comparative method of data analysis. To summarize,

- Early in data collection, the researcher formulates general definitions of the social phenomenon.
- He or she holds these definitions up to data as they are collected.
- The definitions are modified to accommodate new data that do not fit them.
- The researcher intentionally seeks cases that do not fit current definitions.
- He or she formulates a definition that provides a universal explanation of the data.

As data are collected and analyzed, a researcher may discover that the emerging explanation does not account for all instances. At this point, the researcher could choose to narrow or shift the focus of the study. For example, an observer of students in an introductory math course may be guided by a research question about the students' relationship with the faculty member.

Early data collection might reveal, however, that the relationship that predominates is among students divided into groups by ethnicity and age. This dominant story shifts the research question and the focus of data collection and analysis. In marginalia on field notes and through research memos written later, this researcher begins to code data related to the dominant story—student groups.

Qualitative research codes generally fall into several broad categories, including setting or context; definition of the situation; participant perspective, including the participants' ways of thinking about other people and objects; process and activity that describe a single event or series of events; strategy; relationship and social structure; and methods. A basic description of these codes is offered by Bogdan and Biklen (1998), with more exhaustive treatment of coding and other data analysis techniques provided by Auerbach and Silverstein (2003) and Miles and Huberman (1994).

To ease the burden of data reduction, particularly coding, researchers are increasingly relying on qualitative data analysis software packages as noted earlier. A word of caution is warranted here. Qualitative researchers must immerse themselves in their data to extract meaning from it. This is an intellectual and mechanical process that software packages can aid but they are not likely to be a replacement for human decision making. Before spending time and resources on these packages, understand their purposes and their limitations.

Generalizability, Validity, and Reliability in Qualitative Research

Standard qualitative research terms such as generalizability, validity, and reliability do not apply to qualitative research. Rather, qualitative researchers must present their approach and design in a way to assure readers of its soundness or trustworthiness. Some concern themselves with, and describe in detail, how findings in one setting (e.g., one summer bridge program at a predominantly White, urban, selective institution) can be transferable to other settings, such as similar programs at other predominantly white, urban, selective institutions. Another qualitative researcher may be interested in how findings from this study of participants in a summer bridge program can be generalized to other groups where new members of a community share an unfamiliar and intense experience, for example soldiers at boot camp. Chaskes' (1996) study of first-year students as immigrants is a good example of the transferability of the research from one type of group (immigrants) to another (first-year college students).

Another term that may be used for generalizability in qualitative research is credibility (i.e., how confident one can be that what the researcher has purported to study is actually studied and how trustworthy the findings of the original study are for explaining the actions of individuals or groups in another setting). Credibility is of concern to the qualitative researcher who is conducting a study that is intended to generate a theory of social phenomenon beyond one setting (which is not always the case). Internal validity—whether the findings seem credible to the research's participants and consumers—is always relevant. The qualitative researcher's task is to guard against threats to the trustworthiness of their study's findings through, most importantly, self-awareness or reflexivity. Other strategies for promoting trustworthiness in qualitative research validity include extending fieldwork, assigning easy-to-understand descriptors to the data, asking participants for feedback, triangulating the data (i.e., using two or more methods to collect data to strengthen validity of the study), asking for peer review or external audit, seeking out data that do not fit the emerging model, pattern matching across data, and ruling out alternative explanations (Johnson & Christensen, 2008).

Unlike credibility, reliability in qualitative research is often considered of dubious helpfulness. Reliability, or the degree to which one study can be exactly replicated by another researcher, contradicts a primary feature of qualitative research—that the researcher is the instrument. Qualitative researchers give a nod to reliability by being thorough in their description of the perspective (including biases) they bring to a study. In this way, a researcher conducting a follow-up study receives fair warning about how the original researcher's perspective may have focused the study design, data collection, and analysis. If the original researcher is a student leadership practitioner and the follow-up researcher is an English faculty member, the likelihood that they would wish to study the same social phenomenon in the same way is small. This overt description of the researcher's perspective and how it might shape the research is a strength of the qualitative approach.

Writing the Report

Chapter 5 of this book details the conventions of various outlets available for disseminating research, including peer-reviewed journals, books, periodicals, newsletters, and listservs. In venues calling for a lengthy treatment, the writer will include all sections used in the research proposal from statement of the problem and purpose of the study to conclusions and implications for future research and practice. For these venues, qualitative research reports are written in narrative form with direct quotes from the data serving as evidence to support the researcher's emergent theory or conclusions. The source of the data (e.g., observations, interviews, focus groups) is not typically identified in the narrative and every theme or subtheme is accompanied by two or more data points. Whether the end product is an internal report or a study for submission to a peer-reviewed journal, the display of data organized around the analytical framework is the centerpiece. All other aspects of the write-up, from the introduction and literature review to the conclusion, are built to support and reflect this section.

Conclusion

This chapter began with a discussion of the characteristics of a successful qualitative researcher, including self-awareness, writing and listening skills, empathy, patience, organizational skills, analytical abilities, and flexibility. Without these characteristics, strict attention to every technique described after that is made much more difficult. Qualitative research on students in transition can be an exhausting, exhilarating, and, ultimately, valuable form of public service. Being an instrument of research gives the qualitative scholar a powerful, and often deeply personal, opportunity to understand, and explain social phenomenon. As personal as qualitative research on students in transition may be, it is also a strict scholarly undertaking with conventions established over several decades of practice. Qualitative researchers who understand and adhere to these conventions enjoy the greatest number of opportunities to share their research and to impact the lives of college students in transition.

CHAPTER 4
CONDUCTING QUANTITATIVE RESEARCH ON COLLEGE STUDENT TRANSITIONS

As discussed in chapter 2, the primary purpose of quantitative research is to draw from the existing body of knowledge and theory in order to examine relationships among measurable conditions. Evidence about these relationships are then used to advance our understanding about the cause and effect of events as well as to be able to predict the outcome of similar events in the future under like conditions (Creswell, 2009; Merriam & Simpson, 2000). Quantitative studies tend to be rooted in positivist or postpositivist approaches and assumptions about human behavior. Positivism holds that "features in the social environment constitute an objective, independent reality and are relatively constant across time and settings" (Gall, Borg, & Gall, 1996, p. 28) and is the foundation for the traditional scientific method. Postpositivism is not quite as deterministic as positivism. Although it still maintains the notion of an objective truth, it asserts that researchers cannot know this truth entirely but can only conjecture about how closely their findings represent it.

Higher education scholars will generally select a quantitative methodology when their research goal is to test theory or to explain the outcomes of student experiences, programs, and pedagogy. The broad scope and generalizability of quantitative approaches also tend to make them more attractive to researchers focused on understanding the breadth of the research topic under study. The quantitative researcher studying college students in transition strives to explain why and under what conditions initiatives such as first-year seminars, service-learning experiences, or peer mentoring programs are effective for new student adjustment and success. Further, they seek to extend and apply the lessons learned from their research to other programs, groups of students, or institutional settings.

When compared to the purposes and characteristics of qualitative research outlined in the previous chapter, it is clear that quantitative methodology is quite different from that approach. It is, therefore, not surprising that the role and disposition of a researcher using this methodology also tends to be different than those of qualitative researchers. Further, successful quantitative researchers usually share several traits: (a) strong mathematical or statistical abilities, (b) planfulness, (c) objectivity, (d) ability to see the big picture, and (e) strong technical writing abilities.

Strong mathematical or statistical abilities. The primary language of quantitative research is numeric. As the name implies, research conducted in this methodological tradition is focused on quantifying human behavior and experiences. This focus on observation and measurement tends to draw researchers who have a facility with numbers and math. Although formalized training is helpful in conducting quantitative studies, knowledge of specific statistical techniques and methods is less important than a natural tendency to view complex phenomena as the sum of measurable components and a comfort with numbers.

Planfulness. The process of quantitative research is determined a priori and then follows a fairly prescriptive research path. Researchers often carefully review the literature to inform the purpose of their study and determine research questions. Survey instruments and other methods are developed and fully vetted in advance of data collection and remain unchanged throughout the research process. The focus of the study, relationships between variables, and even expected outcomes of the research are all considered and posited before the study is conducted. As such, successful quantitative researchers are able to consider and plan for all elements of the research beforehand and then effectively manage the execution of that plan.

Objectivity. Unlike qualitative researchers, who are themselves the instrument of data collection, quantitative researchers' role in the research process is intentionally distant from the participants in the study. They may be the architects of the research study, but quantitative researchers are intentional in their efforts to minimize the bias of their beliefs or involvement in the research design as well as in the collection and analysis of the data. Most often, they mediate their impact on the study process through the planful identification and execution of the research process. However, throughout the study, it is critical that quantitative researchers hold themselves accountable by frequently checking their objective position.

Ability to see the big picture. Given the intent for the findings of quantitative studies to be generalizable, the object of study is usually a large group of subjects, typically known as a sample, who are intended to be representative of all subjects who share the same characteristics (i.e., the population). The scope of quantitative research tends to be large and focused on breadth rather than depth. Further, quantitative research emphasizes the product rather than the process. Thus, it is more critical to the success of this type of research to be able to aggregate individual elements together and draw a meaningful conclusion about the big picture.

Strong technical writing abilities. It is important to be able to capture all of the highly analytical elements of the quantitative research design as well as to effectively communicate numeric data and associated conclusions. If quantitative researchers want their work to contribute to higher education scholarship, theory, and practice, they must be able to communicate complex technical ideas in simple and accessible terms to their audience(s). Therefore, strong technical writing skills are critical to the success of any quantitative research project.

Where to Begin: Clarifying the Purpose of the Study

The previous chapters identified the process of framing and identifying the research question, which, in turn, guides the researcher to the appropriate methodology for that scholarly issue within the field of the first-year experience and students in transition. A critical step in the design of a research study is to acknowledge the researcher's assumptions and expectations for the scholarly work and to identify the goals and intended outcomes of the study. In quantitative methodology, this process is most often addressed through the statement of purpose for a study and/or through the development of research hypotheses. Both of these approaches are informed by existing theory related to the topic of interest, draw upon findings from the body of extant knowledge on the issue under study, and consider the conditions of the current research. In other words, the assumptions, expectations, and potential outcomes articulated in the purpose statement or hypotheses are not arbitrary but, rather, represent thoughtful consideration and educated speculation.

A statement of purpose is a common section of most quantitative theses, dissertations, and scholarly articles. It is usually found at the end of the review of relevant literature and theory or in its own section immediately thereafter. This placement in the final written product of a research study aptly represents where the development of a purpose statement falls in the research process. Throughout the review of previous research studies and related theoretical literature, it is likely that researchers are forming some notion of how the current work will fit into the larger body of knowledge on this topic. Developing that notion from its early phase to a fully conceptualized inquiry statement is at the core of the purpose statement.

The articulation of purpose does not need to be long, but it does need to include the research question(s) and a statement of how the current study intends to contribute to the field. In quantitative work, the purpose is often informed by gaps in previous research or questions that emerged from past studies. For example, Hofer's (2008) research on the impact of parent/child relationships and technology on college transitions represented this approach: "The initial study addressed the first semester of college only, and considerably more research is needed. The project reported here...[examines] how technological changes influence development across the college years" (p. 11). In addition, purpose statements can be informed by theory as in the case of Weissman and Magill's (2008) article in which they drew from Astin's Inputs-Environment-Outcomes model to inform their study: "In applying Astin's model to first-year seminars, ...some students may benefit from one type of first-year seminar while similar results may be attained for other students who experience a different type of seminar" (p. 67).

Another way to articulate the expectations and contributions of one's scholarly work is through hypotheses. A hypothesis is a tentative statement about the expected findings of the study that will be subjected to empirical testing in the current research project. While it may be used in place of or as a complement to a purpose statement, a hypothesis is often narrower in scope and represents a very specific statement of expected outcomes from the research question rather than general guidelines for the work. For example, in their work on cocurricular involvement and first-year transition,

Tieu and Prancer (2009) could have articulated the research question: How does cocurricular involvement affect first-year adjustment to the university? Instead, they articulated much more specific outcomes for their work, hypothesizing "that involvement (measured in terms of both its quantity and quality) would be related to adjustment to university, and that this relationship would be mediated by self-esteem, stress, social support, and social skills" (p. 47). Because of its specificity, hypothesis testing requires a solid theoretical foundation and a deep literature base and is generally a better fit for very directed approaches rather than more exploratory analyses in quantitative research.

While both statements of purpose and hypotheses do have some important differences, they both provide a rationale, direction, and parameters for the research process. Their development is an important early step in quantitative work. The following questions may help guide the development of statements of purpose or hypotheses:

- What were the most important findings from the examination of research and theory on the topic of interest? What is missing? Based on this information, what questions still need to be answered?
- What were the most important questions generated by the previous work? Why is it important to learn the answers to these questions?
- Given (a) the information learned from a review of the theory and literature on the topic of interest and (b) the conditions of the current study, what is likely to be the outcome of the study? What is the basis of this prediction?
- Are there specific issues and relationships an informed person would expect to emerge from the current study? What are they?

Definition and Identification of Variables

When discussing quantitative approaches to research, it is important to understand how to identify and categorize elements, conditions, and events within higher education. In quantitative methods, the term variable is used to describe these building blocks of the research study. A variable is any measurable characteristic or attribute of an individual or organization that can take on a range of values within the group or organization being studied (Bordens & Abbot, 1991; Creswell, 2009; Jaeger, 1993). Although the empirical study of students and higher education is extremely complex, quantitative research can be distilled into the relationship between two primary classes of variables: independent and dependent. Further, these variables are typically arranged in a temporal sequence for the research study.

Dependent variables represent the primary issue or outcome of interest in a quantitative research study. The value or variation of the dependent variable, due to the influence or association of one or more educational conditions or student characteristics, is the primary focus of quantitative research and often the foundation of the research question(s), purpose statement, and hypotheses. In most instances, there is one dependent variable in a quantitative study, although a researcher may choose to include several measures of that variable to validate their findings. Common examples of dependent variables in quantitative work conducted on students in transition are retention, satisfaction, integration, persistence, cognitive and affective development, and the establishment of interpersonal relationships. Dependent variables are also called outcome or effect variables.

Independent variables represent the conditions or characteristics that can influence, affect, and, potentially, cause outcomes. Because of their place in the temporal sequence, they are sometimes referred to as antecedent or predictor variables. Since in certain research designs independent variables can be manipulated, they can also be called treatment variables. While there may be a particular independent variable of interest in a study, researchers often include several of these types of variables to be able to adequately measure the complexity of the college student experience. Examples of independent variables in the first-year experience and students in transition field include students' background characteristics; previous educational experiences and preparation; involvement in programs and activities; use of campus services; participation in curricular interventions such as service-learning, first-year seminars, learning communities, Supplemental Instruction, and other academic support initiatives; and relationships with peers, faculty, staff, families, and advisors.

While independent variables represent a large category of educational phenomena that can impact the dependent variable, there are different kinds of independent variables that are useful when conducting research of undergraduate students' experiences and outcomes. One type of independent variable is a control variable, which represents antecedents other than the primary independent variable of interest for the research question "that researchers measure because they potentially influence the dependent variable" (Creswell, 2009, p. 51). Thus, the influence of control variables may detract from the researcher's understanding of the relationship between the primary independent variable(s) of interest and the dependent variable. Therefore, the researcher must statistically control for the influence of these variables on the dependent variable in order to find the most probable answer to the research question for the study. Control variables are often demographic characteristics or aspects of the institutional environment that are highly associated with the independent variable(s) of interest, the outcome variable, or both. For example, when looking at the impact of first-year seminar participation (i.e., the independent variable) on grade point average (i.e., the dependent variable), it is important to consider both students' previous academic performance and any self-selection into the course, which represent control variables. If the researcher did not account for the impact of these variables, it would be possible to attribute higher grades to seminar participation when, in fact, it may only represent the tendency for more academically conscientious and higher-performing students to sign up for first-year seminars.

Mediating variables represent another type of independent variable that stand between the independent variable of interest and the dependent variable. Similar to control variables, they often have a positive relationship with the primary independent variable(s) of interest, the dependent variable, or both. However, rather than controlling for their influence on the other variables in the temporal sequence, researchers use mediating variables to help explain the relationship between the independent variable(s) of interest and the dependent variable. These are often experiences that are associated with the independent variable and facilitate the ultimate impact on the dependent variable. For example, academic engagement, social integration, and student satisfaction are three common mediating variables in retention studies. So, the independent variable of interest in a retention study (e.g., student experience, characteristics, or participation in various first-year initiatives or interventions) can enhance satisfaction, integration, and/or engagement (i.e., mediating variables), which, in turn, lead(s) to greater persistence.

The research question, statement of purpose, and hypotheses should reflect both the dependent variable and the primary independent variable(s) of interest. Much like one can diagram sentences to find the object and subject, it should be possible to identify the critical variables of a study from the quantitative research questions and/or hypotheses. For example, Miller, Janz, and Chen (2007) proposed several research questions that each communicated information about the independent and dependent variables in the study. The first question, "Is there a significant effect on [the] retention level for students of high, middle, and low levels of pre-college academic preparation?" (p. 52), clearly articulates retention as the dependent variable and academic preparation as the independent variable of interest. In their second question, "Is there a significant effect on retention level for students who participate in a first-year seminar versus those who do not?" (p. 52), retention remains the dependent variable, but they introduce participation in a first-year seminar as another independent variable of interest in their research.

It is important to be able to articulate the primary variables of interest at an early stage of the research process. What is the dependent variable? What independent variables are included in the study? It is advisable to review the research question(s), hypotheses, and purpose statement to see if they adequately reflect the primary independent and dependent variables of focus for the research study.

Identifying Sources of Data and Participants

Identifying a source of data is a critical step in the quantitative research process. In this process, researchers are finding an access point to the population of interest and creating the means to collect data from members of that population. As mentioned above, the power of the sample, or subset of the population that participates in the quantitative research study, to draw meaningful conclusions about the population and, thus, answer the research question(s), is largely dependent upon how it is designated and drawn.

One of the first decisions at this stage of the quantitative research is whether there is an option to fulfill the goals of the research as articulated in the purpose statement by using previously collected data or whether it is necessary to collect original data for the study. If existing data are available on the topic of interest, the benefits to using it in what is commonly known as secondary data analyses, is that it saves significant investment of resources, most notably time, that the data collection phase of research can take. However, the primary limitation of this approach is that the data source was not specifically designed for the particular research needs of the current study and, thus, may not define variables in ways that are most meaningful, contain certain questions of interest, or include students within the sample that would best fit the current research. In other words, previously collected data really represent a hand-me-down, and researchers who use them in secondary data analyses must take them as they are. Conversely, the benefit of using original data is that researcher will have ultimate control over all aspects of the data collection process, such as survey design, sampling techniques, participation recruitment strategies, and experimental design. However, each of those steps in the process of designing the conditions and tools for data collection can be extremely labor, time, and cost intensive. Given these considerations, the flexibility of exploratory analyses tend to lend themselves more toward the use of existing data, while the specificity of hypothesis-testing may demand research conditions that can only be achieved in the collection of original data.

To fully consider the benefits and limitations of secondary data analyses, it is a useful exercise to conduct a thorough and systematic review of data resources or a data audit as part of the research process. Over the past few decades, there has been a proliferation of off-the-shelf research and assessment tools that collect very useful national data to study the first-year experience and students in transition. Some examples include the

- College Student Experiences Questionnaire (CSEQ)
- College Student Expectations Questionnaire (CSXQ)
- Community College Survey of Student Engagement (CCSSE)
- Cooperative Institutional Research Program's (CIRP)
  - Freshman Survey
  - Your First College Year (YFCY) survey
  - College Senior Survey (CSS)
- First-Year Initiative (FYI) benchmarking survey
- Learning and Study Strategies Inventory (LASSI)
- National Survey of Student Engagement (NSSE)
- Perceptions, Expectations, Emotions and Knowledge (PEEK) About College assessment tool
- Survey of Entering Student Engagement (SENSE)

These instruments create a virtual alphabet soup of research opportunities (Swing, 2004). Many of the entities that sponsor and support the national administration of these surveys (e.g., the Higher Education Research Institute at UCLA, the Center for Postsecondary Research at Indiana University, Educational Benchmarking Incorporated) have procedures for external researchers to request access to data in order to pursue original research studies and, thus, provide valuable sources for secondary data analyses for quantitative research.

In addition to utilizing data from national surveys, campuses and systems of higher education house huge amounts of data on students. In the past few decades, the accountability movement in higher education has grown to the point that collecting and reporting data on college students has become an expected activity for any institution of higher education. From the admissions process to graduation, institutions are constantly capturing information about their students that range from grades in classes that count toward their major to the number of times they visit campus recreation facilities. While the use of systemwide or institutional data may slightly limit the generalizability of research findings only to other institutions of similar type and characteristics, the availability and sheer volume of these data make any institution a virtual clearinghouse of quantitative information on undergraduate students' experiences, transition, and outcomes.

If the research question and purpose for a new study do not fit with previously collected data or a researcher is not willing to accept the limitations of secondary data analyses, the next phase of any quantitative study is to create a data collection tool most often through the development of a survey. There are numerous resources on the development of questionnaires for survey research (e.g., De Leeuw, Hox, & Dillman, 2008; Fowler, 1995; Rea & Parker, 1997; Suskie, 1996), and a thorough treatment of survey design considerations and strategies is well beyond the scope of this introductory text. However, there are certain common aspects to survey design that provide a foundation for greater understanding of quantitative research.

On a very basic level, a researcher should strive for validity and reliability in the construction of a data collection instrument for the research question under study. While validity is a complex measurement concept, ultimately a valid "instrument actually measures what it purports to measure" (Jaeger, 1993, p. 384). Validity is not an absolute measure, but Suskie (1996) aligns it closely with the concept of truthfulness; "if a questionnaire is valid, you are finding out what respondents really, truthfully think about what you really, truthfully want to know" (p. 56). Reliability is a measurement construct that refers to a survey's consistency; "a measurement instrument that is reliable will provide consistent results when a given individual is measured repeatedly under near-identical conditions" (Jaeger, p. 379). A good survey is one that actually measures the issues of interest to the study (validity) and does so in a consistent fashion (reliability), thus generating relevant and trustworthy data for the research study.

Beyond these basic tenets, researchers also want to be sure to develop a survey instrument with the research subject in mind as well as the goals of the study. Questions should be clear and use language that is understandable to the target population. It is important that each item measure only a single construct of interest to the study and that the instrument does not include jargon or slang. Response options to questions should be meaningful, appropriate for the question, and organized into measurable and consistent scales. Finally, while it is always enticing to add just one more item to the instrument, curbing survey length should be a consideration. Not only is it respectful to the research subjects and their time to administer a survey of reasonable length, but a shorter, more focused instrument is more likely to encourage participation in the study, thereby increasing the response rate (i.e., the proportion of the population that participates in the study) and sample size for the research study. Given the number of issues to consider in the construction of a high-quality instrument for quantitative research, it is common practice to conduct a practice round of data collection, also known as a pilot study, to test and refine the data collection tool.

Once a survey instrument has been developed and tested, it is time to identify and recruit the participants for the study who will then respond to the survey, generating the data for analyses. Most quantitative research studies have a group of students in mind for the work. This group is often determined by the purpose statement and dependent and independent variables. For example, in Black and Voelker's (2008, p. 29) study on peer leaders, they asked, "Is having a preceptor in an introductory course [at the University of Hartford] associated with increased engagement...among first-year students?" From this research question, it is possible to determine that all first-year students at the University of Hartford are the general focus of study and that students in an introductory course with a preceptor are of particular interest to the researchers.

When identifying participants for a quantitative research study, typically referred to as subjects, it is first important to understand the overarching group from which participants can be drawn to engage in the study. This body of subjects represents the population for a quantitative research project. More specifically, the population for a study includes "all individuals making up a group of interest in a study" (Bordens & Abbot, 1991, p. G-12). While on the surface this may seem to be an easy exercise, it can be difficult to set appropriate parameters for the population in a quantitative research study. For instance, using Black and Voelker's (2008) study as an example, one could posit that the population is all first-year students without limiting it to the institution of interest to the researchers or to identify the population as *all* students at the university, rather than understanding that only first-year students, and especially first-year students in introductory courses, represent the group of interest for that study. Another common mistake is to define the population too narrowly, such as first-year students in classes with preceptors. While that may be the independent variable of interest for Black and Voelker, their research question indicated an intent to make a statement about the influence of preceptors on first-year student engagement in introductory courses. Their interest in comparing the experiences across treatment groups (i.e., students with a preceptor in their class versus those in classes without preceptors) suggests that the population is all first-year students enrolled in introductory courses at the University of Hartford.

The population of many studies is quite a large group of potential participants. While it is certainly possible to capture data from every member of the population, it is usually improbable and should not necessarily represent a goal of the quantitative researcher. Instead, the intent should be to capture a subset of the population, or sample, that is powerful enough to yield findings and conclusions that are meaningful and reasonable for the population under study. A few key factors that contribute to the power of a sample are size (how close you are to capturing the entire population?), representativeness (how similar the subset of subjects are to the population with respect to key characteristics?), and the limitation of bias (what attempts did you make to limit all of the confounding[1] influences in the data collection?). Various quantitative sampling techniques attempt to capitalize on these aspects of power to yield a meaningful sample for the study.

The most general approach to identifying participants is a population sample, which means that the goal of the researcher is to give every subject in the population the opportunity to participate in the study. This method has the potential to maximize the size of the sample if the researcher is able to generate enough response to the data collection effort. The greater this response, the more likely the sample is to represent the population and, thus, further increase the power of the sample. However, unless students are required to participate in the study, it is likely that the researcher's efforts will yield less than 100% participation. Therefore, it is important to understand how those individuals who responded to the data collection efforts are different from those who did not. If there are common patterns of difference between these two groups, it is likely that the sample suffers from nonresponse bias and may have limitations in its representativeness of the population. Although population sampling is often very labor, time, and resource intensive, it does have the potential to yield the largest response rate and most powerful sample for use in a quantitative study.

While population sampling has the potential to include every possible participant, a random sample represents an intentional subset of the population that is drawn such that "every member of the population has an equal opportunity to be included in the sample" (Bordens & Abbot, 1991, p. G-13). Many databases and statistical programs have the ability to generate a random sample of names so creating such a sample from the population, once identified, is often quite simple. Since the inclusion of a subject in a random sample is based on chance alone and not on any targeted recruitment attempts, random sampling eliminates certain biases that may emerge from students volunteering for the study (i.e., self-selection bias) or from any bias inherent in the researcher's recruitment methods (e.g., sampling based on

---

[1] Confounding variables are similar to control variables in that their association with the independent variable of interest and/or the dependent variable can introduce bias into the study. However, their influence cannot be directly measured or accounted for in the way that control variables can be. Researchers can only speculate about the role and influence of confounding variables on the findings of the study.

proximity or via recommendation, such as with snowball sampling[2]). While the final sample is likely to be much smaller than for population sampling, random sampling has the benefit that it is often more manageable than population sampling and still has the potential to capture a wide range of data points that are relevant to the population.

Similar to population sampling, random sampling techniques are still subject to nonresponse bias, which can affect the representativeness of the sample. However, unlike population sampling, there is a specific strategy often used in random sampling to help increase the representativeness of the final sample. If the researcher is aware that the population is very diverse and/or that there is a history of nonresponse bias for particular groups within the population, it may be important to modify the random sampling slightly. In a stratified random sample, the population is parsed into groups based upon certain characteristics, and then random sampling is assigned within each group such that a subset of students from each group identified in the sampling process has an equal chance of being represented in the final sample. For example, this technique may be useful to researchers who are working with racially diverse populations of students in transition in which underrepresented groups have a history of lower response rates.

Finally, there are instances in quantitative research when a targeted sampling technique is used. Targeted sampling techniques are intentionally biased data collection methods that can help increase the representation of particular members of the population. This may include oversampling certain groups after stratifying the population by using targeted incentive programs or enhanced recruitment efforts. In some instances, this method is employed to help overcome historic nonresponse bias among certain groups, such as students of color, students with lower grades, and nonresidential students, in order to generate a more representative sample. In other instances, quantitative research questions focus on a particular intervention or student transition experience and more pointed sampling efforts may be needed to recruit students engaged in the program, service, or experience of interest. In any event, it is important to note that despite the final result, whether

---

[2] Snowball sampling is a technique in which participants help the researcher identify other similar participants; often used when the research topic is controversial or a specific population of participants is difficult to find (Keyton, 2006).

it be a representative sample or one inclusive of the treatment variable, the researcher has introduced bias into the study through the use of a targeted sample, which needs to be considered in the analysis and interpretation of the data collected from that sample.

While the above techniques are intended to increase the power of the sample through careful design a priori, it is still possible to generate a small, unrepresentative, or biased sample. If this is the case, there are a few means to address these limitations even after the sample has been drawn. For instance, some researchers choose to replace missing values in the dataset via statistical means to enhance the usable number of cases and the size of their sample (Allison, 2001; Croninger & Douglas, 2005; Volkwein & Yin, 2010). Another option would be to include or exclude specific cases in the initial sample to create a modified, albeit smaller, sample that is more representative of the population of interest. Yet another example includes the use of statistical weights in the sample such that those cases from underrepresented and overrepresented groups are equalized in the sample to approximate representativeness (Thomas, Heck, & Bauer, 2005; Volkwein & Yin). Each of these modifications has the potential to introduce more bias and confounding influences so they should be used with caution. However, it may be prudent for a researcher to consider this trade-off in light of the gains to be had with a more representative and larger sample.

Research Design and Statistical Methods

All research approaches and data analysis decisions generally serve one of two goals of quantitative research. First, quantitative work can examine the characteristics and potential relationships between various elements, conditions, and phenomena (i.e., variables in higher education), which is done through exploratory analyses. Second, quantitative inquiry attempts to identify and evaluate potential explanations for relationships between variables (Bordens & Abbot, 1991), which is most frequently represented through hypothesis testing. While both provide our field with important information, they differ in purpose, sophistication, and meaning. Elements of research design and the selection of statistical methods help address the different goals of quantitative research and frame the study appropriately to achieve its purposes.

Research Design

In its most basic form, quantitative research is intended to test assumptions, often articulated as hypotheses, or gather new information by manipulating as many aspects of the treatment and groups under study as possible. In an experimental research design, this often happens through the random assignment of study participants to specific groups or by controlling for all elements of an experience. However, it is not usually reasonable or ethical to exert such tight control on students and their choices within their educational experience. In fact, the diversity of students; the variety of institutional type, setting, and control; and the broad range of student experiences is a hallmark of American higher education. As such, experimental design is quite rare in quantitative studies of students in transition. Instead, quasi-experimental designs, in which students are not randomly assigned and researchers work within the educational conditions that exist for the students, are far more common.

Most individuals who research topics related to students in transition are interested in student change and development, often as a result of a particular student experience, service, program, condition, or intervention. Since time is a necessary element of change and development, it is important to understand two commonly used quasi-experimental research designs that focus on understanding change over time: (a) cross-sectional and (b) longitudinal study designs.

Cross-sectional research designs are ones in which two or more groups are selected across developmental conditions. For example, if a researcher is interested in studying specific elements of the first-year experience in a cross-sectional design, she may select a group of first-year students and a group of seniors who are as similar in personal characteristics as possible. Comparisons would then be made across the two groups to ascertain changes in the outcomes of interest that can be attributed to the college experience and the significant transitions therein. The primary benefit of a cross-sectional design to study the development of students is that one does not actually have to wait for time to pass in order to study impact. Conversely, the challenge of these designs is that there are numerous other variables that can explain the difference between the two groups, which cannot always be effectively controlled in the research study. Therefore, it can be difficult to attribute change in the outcome to the independent variable of interest.

Other researchers prefer designs that compare scores on the outcomes of interest that are taken from the same group of students before and after the student's participation in a course, program, or intervention, which represents a longitudinal research design. Since the same group of participants remains the focus of the study, many of the confounding effects of background and other characteristics are controlled in a longitudinal study, and the effect of the independent variable on the outcome is more easily isolated and analyzed. However, since the researcher must allow for students' participation in the treatment as well as the opportunity for it to have an effect, longitudinal studies can take a long time to conduct. Further, a pre-posttest design requires more than one point of data collection, which can double the administrative challenges of gathering original data, requires that data from the multiple collection points be matched, and introduces the possibility that students may not participate in both data collection opportunities.

Statistical Methods

Descriptive statistical approaches attempt to tabulate, summarize, and organize data for the purpose of describing the group from which they were collected. This class of statistics does not generally attempt to analyze these data or relationships between variables for explanations of impact and are more frequently used for exploratory analyses or as an initial step in hypothesis testing. Dependent and independent variables and their temporal sequence are not usually considered in descriptive analyses. Some common examples of descriptive statistics are

- *Measures of central tendency, such as means, medians, and modes.* These statistics use one measurement to communicate the center of the distribution of scores or measures on a variable. For instance, it may be critical to a researcher's understanding of her or his study to calculate average student participation rates in first-year seminars, service-learning, and learning communities among the group that is being studied.
- *Measures of variation, including variance, standard deviation, and frequency distributions.* Rather than collapsing all of the scores into one summary statistic as with measures of central tendency, measures of variation provide additional information about the range of scores across the categories of measurement. For instance, a researcher could

investigate the distribution of students across GPA categories as it relates to understanding student success within a study. In another example, it might be useful to examine how new students spend their time on a variety of activities in a week as reported on an hours-per-week scale.

- *Measures of association, most notably correlations.* Correlations measure the linear relationship between two variables to determine if they are significantly dependent from a statistical perspective. It is important to note that this statistical dependency does not suggest directionality or causality; it only means that the two variables are, in fact, associated with one another. For example, it may be tempting to say that because participation in first-year seminars has a strong positive relationship with students' GPA that their participation in this course is the reason for their academic achievement. However, as mentioned in the earlier discussion of control variables, it is also as likely that that those students who elect to participate in first-year seminars have a history of higher academic achievement than those who do not or that the seminar itself generally yields a higher grade, thus inflating the GPAs for those students participating in the seminar.

Although they are limited in their ability to identify causality and directionality, descriptive statistics are extremely informative and useful in quantitative inquiry and are likely to represent at least a portion of the method for most quantitative studies. The enhanced understanding of key variables that comes from this type of methodological approach is an important first step for researchers who will go on to examine the relationships between these variables as can be seen for numerous studies recently published in the *Journal of The First-Year Experience & Students in Transition* (e.g., Hofer, 2008; McBroom, Fife, & Nelson, 2008; Strayhorn, 2009; Tieu & Prancer, 2009; Walpole et al., 2008). In fact, in some instances, findings from descriptive statistics are the primary contribution of a quantitative research study. This is most often the case for more general research questions, including studies that explore topic areas or groups of students that are still relatively new and not represented in the literature or consider very large groups of students that are widely informative. Some of the most well-known examples of national research studies that draw upon descriptive statistics include the Annual Report of the National Study of Student Engagement (NSSE), the national norms published annually from the Cooperative Institutional Research Program's (CIRP) Freshman Survey, and the results of the National Survey of First-Year Seminars administered on a triennial basis by the National Resource Center for The First-Year Experience and Students in Transition.

Inferential statistics represent the next level of sophistication for understanding characteristics, relationships, and potential causality between variables in quantitative work. While descriptive statistics condense a range of values into statistics that tell the researcher about the qualities of the group from which the data were drawn, inferential statistics attempt to expand those findings and assumptions to make claims about the entire class of individuals that were represented by the group from whom the data were drawn. These analyses will help researchers go beyond questions that ask *what is* and address *what if* or *is it also true* types of research questions. As such, inferential statistics are often used to test specific hypotheses about the characteristics of or relationships between variables.

While there are many types of inferential statistics, some commonly used in first-year experience and students in transition research evaluate the reliability of differences between the average score (i.e., means) of various groups on a particular measure. These groups could represent differences based upon levels of the independent variable of interest in the study (e.g., residential students vs. commuters, learning community participants versus nonparticipants, students enrolled in different types of first-year seminars) or between the characteristics of the individuals in a sample as compared to the characteristics of the larger population for the study. If the research question relates to the difference between two groups, a *t*-test will be a useful statistical tool. If it addresses a cross-comparison of the means for multiple groups, an inferential statistics called an analysis of variance (ANOVA) is used to address the statistical difference for the means of three or more groups.[3] For example, Johnson, Kerr, Gans, and Bierschwale (2009) used *t*-tests to examine differences in adolescents' precollege anxiety and depression between two cohorts of students (i.e., one starting college before 9/11 and one beginning college in the fall of 2001). However, these researchers needed

---

[3] A close cousin of the ANOVA is an analysis of covariance (ANCOVA), which allows researchers to include control variables in the model and then examine the difference in means across multiple groups after controlling for potentially biasing variables.

to use an ANOVA to test their hypotheses about differences in anxiety and depression among both cohorts before and after the students began college (i.e., differences between four means: precollege cohort 1, precollege cohort 2, follow-up cohort 1, and follow-up cohort 2).

Higher educators know that not all areas of interest are able to be articulated via a simple mean. Not all spectrums of choice in higher education fall on an ordinal scale such that higher values are associated with larger amounts and smaller values are associated with lesser amounts (e.g., GPA). Oftentimes, researchers are interested in the outcome of students' decisions between equal-but-different options or categories, such as with residential situations, majors, or types of first-year seminars. In those instances, a chi-squared analysis is the more appropriate inferential statistic since it provides a statistical test of the interdependence between two categorical variables. Weissman and Magill (2008) provide a perfect example of the use of a chi-square statistic when they compared the rate of retention across groups of "students who participated and those who did not participate in U101 and University Inquiry courses during the fall semester" (p. 72).

Multivariate analyses represent the next level of sophistication in methodological approaches. These types of studies take into account the impact of multiple independent variables on the outcome of interest in a quantitative study and the web of relationships therein. Because of the complexity that these methodological approaches are able to consider, they are particularly useful to quantitative scholars whose research questions seek to explain relationships between variables or to address complex issues or experiences in higher education. Given the intricacy and interdependence of conditions inherit in transition experiences, multivariate designs are very helpful and often used in quantitative research on the first-year experience and students in transition.

One of the most common multivariate approaches is regression analysis.[4] The primary goal of regression equations is to explain the variation in the

---

[4] Regression analysis is only one of a number of multivariate methods in higher education research, including path analysis, structural equation modeling, hierarchical linear modeling, decision tree analysis, logistic regression, discriminant analysis, and factor analysis. The selection of a multivariate model is dependent

measure of the dependent variable between participants in the study based upon the effect of important independent variables. In order to achieve this goal, these analyses are able to consider the impact of many different independent variables on an outcome variable in one formula. The purpose of regression analyses is to evaluate the predictive power of each independent variable on the dependent variable and identify the group of independent variables that, in combination, explains the most variation in the dependent variable. However, regression also strives toward parsimony, so it drops variables with statistically insignificant predictive power, yielding a final formula that explains as much as possible about the dependent variable with the least amount of independent variables. Thus, regression analyses provide a lot of explanatory bang for the statistical buck.

In their study on "the connection between loneliness and alcohol use in the first college year" (p. 45), McBroom et al. (2008) included numerous independent variables representing a host of student characteristics and experiences, key measures of environmental context, as well as personal and academic experiences to help explain their outcome of interest: the differences in problems experienced among first-year students as the result of drinking alcohol. As one might expect, not all of the variables initially entered into the equation were a part of the final formula. The final formula included seven independent variables—various measures of demographic characteristics, academic achievement, scores on a loneliness scale, knowledge about alcohol and its effect, and the number of alcoholic drinks per week—to explain 45% of the differences observed among students in the study with respect to the problems they experienced due to drinking alcohol.

Finally, it is important to note that these analytical approaches can, and are, used in combination. In a study examining the impact of first-year seminars on student retention, Strayhorn (2009) used all three types of statistical analysis to address his quantitative research questions:

> First, descriptive statistics were used to calculate the means and standard deviations for all independent and dependent variables included in this

---

upon numerous aspects of the purpose and design of the study, the discussion of which goes beyond the scope of this volume. Coughlin (2005) offers a brief introduction to several of these statistics for research and assessment purposes.

analysis. Independent sample t-tests were used to determine differences between first-year seminar participants and those who did not participate in first-year seminars. Last, hierarchical multiple regression tests were employed to measure the impact of first-year seminar participation on overall satisfaction with college, controlling for differences in race, gender, and academic achievement. (p. 17)

With such a thorough use of all statistical methods, Strayhorn was able to distill the characteristics of the 755 participants in the study into a meaningful profile with descriptive statistics, determine that "first-year seminar participants did not differ from nonparticipants in terms of overall satisfaction with college" (p. 17) via inferential statistics, and conclude that the impact of first-year seminar participation on college outcomes is not consistent across groups of students as defined by gender, race, and academic achievement.

Conclusion

This chapter has introduced the basic tenets and goals of quantitative research as well as common characteristics of successful scholars that rely upon this methodological tradition. Drawing upon this foundation, the building blocks of quantitative inquiry were introduced, including identifying the purpose of the study through research questions and hypotheses, types of variables, data collection options, access to study participants, and an array of research designs and statistical methods. When these elements come together, the quantitative research process can yield significant findings, important conclusions, and profound implications. The products of quantitative research have the potential to challenge what is known about college students and help educators shape undergraduate experiences on a broad scale. When done well, quantitative research has the potential to enhance knowledge and inform programs, policies, and pedagogies that educators use to serve students and contribute to their success.

CHAPTER 5
Publishing Results and Disseminating Findings

Making research results available to others involves writing articles and reports and disseminating findings through publication. Publishing results is a serious responsibility for those whose findings may suggest changes in educational policy and/or practice. Even when research results are disappointing and/or do not support one's hypothesis, access to the results may prevent other educators from replicating unsuccessful or unworkable practices and help guide future scholarly activity. Research projects should be launched with the explicit intent to report out the results in documents for consumption by scholars or practitioners on the researcher's own and other campuses. This chapter provides guidance for writing and publishing research on the college student experience with a particular emphasis on conventions and outlets for publishing on topics related to students in transition. Because the art and craft of writing research reports involves pulling together all aspects of the project, many of the suggestions previously offered in this volume will be reinforced here. Researchers typically seek to publish full reports of their studies in academic journals first. Therefore, these publications will be the initial focus, followed by a discussion of a number of other dissemination venues.

Academic Journals

Author's Guidelines

Before beginning the first draft of a research report intended for an audience that primarily includes other researchers, authors should first obtain author's guidelines from publications that align with their research. Author's guidelines, typically printed in the journal or on the publishing organization's website, provide essential information (e.g., manuscript format, number of copies to be submitted, acceptance criteria). Most academic journals specify requirements for length of the submitted manuscript and will not publish longer articles because of rigid space limitations. Even online-only journals with seemingly limitless room in cyber-space adhere to length conventions. Manuscripts that fail to meet these basic criteria are rejected outright or are returned to the author for revision. The author's guidelines for the *Journal of The First-Year Experience & Students in Transition* are typical of those found in academic journals (Appendix A). Chapter 2 suggests additional journals that are appropriate venues for publishing studies on college student transitions.

Manuscript Style

Education and other social and behavioral science journals often adhere to the most recent edition of the *Publication Manual of the American Psychological Association* (APA Manual) as their style guide. Along with the author's guidelines for the journal of interest, the *APA Manual* is an important companion when writing the results of a research project. The *APA Manual* prescribes text and graphic formats, language use, and citation styles, and offers advice on ethical considerations and nonbiased writing. Quantitative and qualitative researchers typically follow a standard format for the research report comprised of seven sections: (a) title page, (b) abstract, (c) introduction, (d) method, (e) results, (f) discussion, and (g) references. Most campus bookstores carry copies of the *APA Manual*, or it can be purchased through booksellers online. APA also offers a pocket guide entitled *Concise Rules of APA Style* (APA, 2005) and *Presenting Your Findings* (Nicol & Pexman, 2010), a guide specific to creating tables and other graphic elements.

Dissecting the Academic Journal Review Process

Researchers who successfully publish in academic journals are intimately familiar with author's guidelines, the *APA Manual*, and the form used by reviewers to determine whether manuscripts are (a) fully accepted, (b) conditionally accepted pending revisions, (c) recommended for revision and resubmission, or (d) rejected. While the review form is as important as the author's guidelines and *APA Manual*, it is often overlooked by researchers and those who provide them with advice. The websites of education journals, such as *The Review of Higher Education* and *The Journal of Higher Education*, offer online guidelines for contributors that may mirror the criteria on a reviewer's form, with some slight variation. If possible, it is advisable to obtain a copy of the review form or the author's checklist for submission, which may also reflect the criteria reviewers use in conducting their reviews. Another helpful resource is the APA Authors and Reviewers Resource site (Appendix A). For most scholars, journal reviewers are their first, and often most critical, audience and serve as gatekeepers to publication. In our opinion, understanding what reviewers seek in a research manuscript is the key to that gate. Offered below is a detailed discussion of the criteria of a typical journal in social science education based on the form used by reviewers for the *Journal of The First-Year Experience & Students in Transition* (Appendix B).

What Matters to Academic Journal Reviewers

Academic journal review forms, like author's guidelines and checklists, all require the author(s) to omit their name(s) from at least one copy of the submitted manuscript. Obviously, institutional affiliations and contact information are also omitted. This will be the manuscript sent to reviewers as part of the blind- or peer-review process, which is intended to be objective.

If a journal editor returns a review form to the author after the manuscript is evaluated, it will not have the reviewer's name on it. Journals each have their own policies regarding returning entire review forms to authors and, if they are returned, the editor is likely to assign a number to each reviewer. The number of reviewers varies by journal. The *Journal of The First-Year Experience & Students in Transition* assigns a typical number, three reviewers, to each manuscript. Whether the journal editor returns the review forms or not, he or she will synthesize the reviews for the author and/or provide the author(s) with salient portions of each review.

Overall Evaluation

Manuscript title. The title of the manuscript (discussed again below) is singularly important. Researchers writing on students in transition should write titles that are straight forward, highly descriptive, and specific to the content of the study. Hollywood titles, those that attempt lyricism or catchiness, should never be used in writing about research on students in transition. "Finding Their Way Home: Listening to the Voices of Students in Their Transitions in and out of College" or "Boys to Men: Fraternity Men Moving From Their First to Second Year," are titles that may be appropriate for other publishing venues (as described later), but academic journal reviewers will likely assume that the author is not writing for an audience interested in scholarship on students in transition. They may, in fact, be harsher on the manuscripts than if they carried titles such as "A Covariate Analysis of Self-Reported Factors Positively and Negatively Impacting Student Transitions at Key Points in the Undergraduate Experience" or "Case Studies of Black Male Rising Sophomore Fraternity Members at Three Predominantly White Institutions of Varying Sizes." These titles suggest that the author(s) understand that scholars are interested in reading studies that use specific types of data collection methods, explore important contexts, employ certain kinds of analytical tools, and draw new and interesting conclusions. Reviewers should not be required to hunt for more than one of these four critical components in a title.

New findings or ideas. The first question reviewers will ask about the study itself is whether the authors have conducted research that fills a gap in the current scholarly understanding of a particular issue. As noted in an earlier chapter, college student transitions have now been studied for nearly three decades, but there are still many questions to be asked and answered. A researcher may be contributing to the scholarship by offering a new method for collecting data, exploring a new approach to serving students in transition, or using a newly designed tool for analyzing data. In the research report, the authors make a convincing argument that they are thoroughly versed in previous scholarly work and have something new to say.

Important findings or ideas. The reviewer of a manuscript submitted to an academic journal will determine if the findings or ideas are not only new but important. The author of a research report must make a case that more than a handful of other scholars or practitioners will benefit from the new understanding they are providing. Understanding the role of seminars for students transferring from community colleges is both new and important because this issue has not received enough scholarly attention and it has implications for thousands of college students and the educators who serve them. A case study of three female seniors involved in a service-learning project who are not representative of an understudied population may be new, but the reviewer will want to know how and to whom it is important.

Compelling rationale for the study. The rationale answers the first So What question about the research project itself. Similar to establishing the importance of understanding a particular issue, authors are charged with providing answers to three questions that underlie this first So What: Why this study, conducted this way, at this time? Answers to these questions signal to the reviewer (and, hopefully, future readers) that of all that could be read on this topic, the results, analysis, and conclusions of this study deserve attention now. A frequently made mistake is to make the claim that a study conducted this way, at this time, is the answer to concerns far outside the scope of the study. We refer to this as the solving-world-hunger problem, by which an author suggests that his or her study is the answer to much that is wrong with higher education. As was discussed earlier under formulating the research question, all but the rarest of studies concern a very small window into understanding students in transition. The reviewer will want to know that the authors have found a compelling reason for conducting their study, but they will also want to know that the author understands that one study is limited in its ability to impact scholarship or work with college students.

Clear writing. Writing for an academic journal is not an opportunity to demonstrate the ability to turn a beautiful phrase as one would when writing poetry or creative prose. Scholars, including journal reviewers, are interested in an unadorned articulation of the reason for the study, the approach used to conduct the study, the analysis of the data, and the conclusions and implications. This is not to suggest that reviewers are seeking wooden language or passively constructed sentences. Good research writing uses the active voice and the third person plural. Writing in the third person singular requires the use of he/she and him/her—awkward terms that can be avoided by use of the third person plural (i.e., they). In writing results of quantitative studies, researchers rarely use the first person (I/we) or second person (you). The rules change for writing reports on qualitative research studies. As Johnson and Christensen (2008) suggest, qualitative researchers themselves are the instruments of research and, therefore, should feel comfortable using the first person (I) in the report, as in "I conducted participant observation in a learning community." Of course, the blind review process and ethical considerations (discussed below) necessitate that all personal identifiers of both the researcher and research participants are removed. The *APA Manual*, again, offers other important suggestions on inclusion, clarity, and other aspects of good academic writing.

Tables and graphs. When narrative will suffice to make an author's point, it should be used. In some instances, especially in quantitative research studies, a table, figure, or other graphic element is necessary to convey an author's meaning. The reviewer's first litmus test where graphic elements are concerned is the question, Is it necessary? After determining need, reviewers will decide if the graphic element is referred to and placed appropriately in the body of the manuscript. They will determine whether the graphic element represents, in the best manner possible, the point the author is attempting to make and may suggest alternative approaches. As with narrative, conventions exist for when to use specific kinds of graphic elements (Nicol & Pexman, 2010). APA guidelines are explicit about design and use of these graphic elements. In qualitative research, quotes are the equivalent of figures and tables and are the data used to illustrate the theory, theme, or thesis that emerged from the research. In qualitative research reports, only those data (e.g., quotes, observations, or data from document collection) that clearly illustrate emergent theories or themes should be included. Likewise, in quantitative research reports, only those data that clearly and succinctly represent the primary findings of the study should be placed in tabular or graphic form. Writing a manuscript for publication in an academic journal is as much about what to leave out as it is what to leave in.

Theory or concept driving the manuscript. The importance of basing a study in existing theory or inside a conceptual framework was established in earlier chapters. As they are with scholarly literature, reviewers are well aware of ideas that have driven and been generated by past research. They will check for an author(s) familiarity with these ideas and how well they have embedded the study in the ideas appropriate to the current inquiry. They will also ask whether the theoretical framework matches the approach to data collection and analysis. A well-crafted research manuscript uses theory at all four important points of a study—rationale, data collection, analysis, and conclusion—to bind the manuscript together.

The reference list. Reviewers reading research reports on students in transition are asked to serve in these capacities because they are well versed in this content area and/or have a solid familiarity with the methods used to conduct studies on these topics. They will know if reference has been made to important past research conducted in the area of a study and whether proper reference has been made to methodologists who have tested the approach used to conduct the study they are reviewing. In terms of mechanics, the reviewers, and later, the editorial staff of a journal, will compare the reference list with every citation in text to ensure exact matches. Every reference in text must also appear in the reference list. On occasion, authors wish to guide their readers to additional sources of information on their topic without linking it directly to their research report. These For Further Reading lists are not part of a manuscript submitted to an academic journal.

Implications for practice. This is the second, critical So What question when writing a research report. Researchers on students in transition are working toward one ultimate goal—understanding and improving the experiences of students at important transitional points in the undergraduate years. This research tradition, starting with researchers such as Paul P. and Dorothy S. Fidler from the University of South Carolina, was founded on making a direct and tangible difference initially in the lives of first-year college students and later in the lives of all students in transition. Reviewers will gauge the impact of the contributions the study has potential to make on the practical, day-to-day work of helping college students achieve their goals. Studies on students in transition are applied research.

However, in the applied nature of this research lies a trap into which too many new researchers fall. This, trap, identified in a previous chapter, is confusing assessment and program evaluation with research. It is enough to say here that research is intended to answer a question many in a scholarly community have and to improve practices across many campuses. If a study is conducted—even one that includes a thorough review of the literature and uses the most sophisticated data collection and analysis tools—to inform educators and improve the student experience on just one campus, or at a limited number of institutions, it is assessment or program evaluation, not research. While extremely, and increasingly valuable, program evaluations and assessments are not appropriate for submission to most academic journals. The audience for implications for practice from a research project is a broad one.

General Organization

Academic journal reviewers are also asked to weigh in on issues of general organization of the manuscript. They will evaluate the quality of the abstract using criteria similar to that of the title: Does it accurately represent and summarize the study, and does it include a summary of the four most important portions of the study: rationale, data collection, analysis, and conclusion? The introduction is intended to clearly describe the purpose and scope of the study with an eye toward replicating the language introduced in the abstract. As part of clear writing, the body of a high-quality manuscript is well organized and rich in the amount and type of detail needed to tell the entire story of the study. Implications for practice, addressed above, must also be accompanied by clear conclusions drawn directly from the analysis and should discuss recommendations for future research that will explore questions related to, but outside the scope of, the current study.

Methodology Review

Researchers who have followed this volume's, or other authors', advice on designing a methodologically sound study should have little trouble writing about the process and procedures they employed to conduct their study. Below are methodological components of a research report of greatest interest to reviewers.

Hypothesis or research question. Reviewers will ask not only if the hypothesis or research question is clearly stated at the beginning of the study, they will determine if it is appropriately referenced at several junctures throughout the report. As indicated earlier, the hypothesis or research question becomes the researcher's mantra, and at every step in the writing process, the investigator should ask, Do these data help answer my research question or relate to my hypothesis?

Sample and sampling methods. While qualitative researchers in social science do not use the language of sampling or sample size, they share with quantitative researchers a concern for the representative nature of the participants in a study. In a report on quantitative research, reviewers want to know who is in the sample under study and why and how it was selected. In qualitative research, the same questions apply: Who were the participants, and why and how were they selected? These questions apply whether the sample or participants represent individuals, groups, or entire institutions. Academic journal reviewers will look carefully for how these issues are addressed.

Measures and treatment procedures. Again, qualitative researchers do not use this exact language to describe the conditions under which their participants were engaged, but they are concerned with the qualitative equivalent—context. In all social science research reports, reviewers will gauge how well an author has described the actions, behaviors, or attitudes of participants under conditions that are either naturally occurring (for most qualitative research) or designed for the study (for most quantitative research). They will also seek a clear description of any tools of measurement used to determine trajectories in actions, behaviors, or attitudes, and treatments applied to an experimental group or withheld from a control group. In research related to students in transition, they will look for a detailed description of a Supplemental Instruction program, for example, when the research concerns some differential achievement level of participants and nonparticipants. The readers' understanding of the measures, treatments, or context in which a study is conducted is central to their ability to determine its applicability to future research and practice.

Research design. As noted earlier, there are times when an author's original research question or hypothesis is impacted by unpredicted changes in the design of the study (i.e., the teachers who were to serve as the gatekeepers for a controlled study on a common critical thinking assignment have a falling out and refuse to participate the week before the study is scheduled to commence). Reviewers working with academic journals are not interested, at least at the point of review, in the messiness that nearly always accompanies the research process. Instead, they will look for a research design that beautifully and intentionally emerged from the research question or hypothesis and will seek to determine if the design is adequate to address the question or hypothesis.

Statistical tests and qualitative analysis approaches. It is standard practice for journal editors to ensure that at least one reviewer assigned to a manuscript is familiar with, if not an expert in, statistical methods or approaches to qualitative data collection and analysis germane to the study under consideration. When writing a research report, the author will carefully describe these components of the project and offer all necessary citations to document that these tests and approaches are appropriate for answering the research question or testing the hypothesis. The reviewer will expect the author to cite previous studies in the field of students in transition or from other social science research that have successfully employed these techniques.

Presentation of findings. As described earlier in the section on graphic elements and display of qualitative data, only those findings that are directly related to answering the research question or addressing the hypothesis should be included. Novice researchers are tempted to create tables for too many aspects of their study, including displays of simple demographic data or limited survey results without statistical analyses and/or including quotes only tangentially related to their research question in qualitative research reports. Journal reviewers and editors offer the following advice when presenting findings that are not clearly related to the research question or hypothesis: When in doubt, leave it out.

Congruence of results, discussion, and recommendations. Academic journal reviewers will determine if the findings of the study are linked to the discussion and can be particularly harsh on manuscripts that include a discussion that takes the reader far afield of the original intent of the research. It is true, though, that very few researchers studying students in transition are steeped exclusively in scholarship: Most are also involved in educational practice. They are advocates, teachers, and administrators with a wide variety of ideas and opinions. The enthusiasm some researchers bring to research on college students lures them into using the research report as an opportunity to discuss a wide range of issues related, even tangentially, to their study and to make recommendations that do not necessarily flow directly from their research findings. The academic journal is not the place for a discussion of the bone one wishes to pick or the editorial one wishes to write.

Relationship between results from current and previous studies. As noted in the discussion of the reference list, academic journal reviewers are selected because they know the literature base. They will determine if, and how well, the findings of the study under review are compared to those of previous research. This also relates to the issues of newness and importance. An author should not be discouraged to find what others conducting very similar studies have found. That is likely an indication that the study was well designed and conducted. If a thorough literature review was undertaken and a genuine need to understand a phenomenon related to students in transition was identified, then a comparison with other studies should reveal at least one new and important contribution made, even if it is to confirm someone else's findings from a previous study.

Significance of contribution. This is the third, and final, So What question in writing the research report. Journal reviewers will want to know if the writer understands and has articulated the depth and breadth of the contribution the research has made, both to the scholarly community and to practitioners. Describing the significance of a study is no time for hyperbole nor is it a time to discount the work that has been done. In this research field, it is an opportunity to clearly and succinctly describe how and how much this study enriches the understanding of college students in transition.

A Final Word About APA Style

The reviewers' first, and last, task is to watch for the manuscript's adherence to APA style. Once an accepted manuscript leaves the reviewers' hands it will pass through several more layers of editing. That said, if an original manuscript includes a nonstandard abstract, is not organized per APA style, has conflicts between in-text and reference list citations, and is written in sexist language (i.e., using the generic *he*), reviewers and editors are much less likely to look kindly upon even the most elegantly conducted study.

After the Review

Once reviewers complete their tasks (which typically take between one and four hours for each manuscript), they return their forms to the editor with recommendations to (a) fully accept the manuscript as written (a rare occurrence), (b) conditionally accept it pending revisions, (c) ask that the manuscript be revised and resubmitted, or (d) reject the manuscript. The time editors give reviewers to return their completed forms ranges from a few weeks to several months, which means that the entire academic journal publication process can take up to a year, depending on the speed of the reviewers and the quality of the manuscript. Online journals with similar review processes may have shorter publication cycles because they are not working with printed material, but reviews of manuscripts submitted to an academic journal of any kind take time. The editorial staff of an academic journal is available to provide information not only on the review and publication cycle, but also on the acceptance rates of manuscripts—often asked as part of the tenure review process for academic faculty.

As noted earlier, once all reviews of a manuscript are returned, the editor will determine next steps. The short letters they write are the acceptance without revision or the rejection. Those letters in between will include both a synthesis of the reviews and/or the review forms themselves and recommendations for addressing the reviewers' comments. The letter may, or may not, include a timeline for return of the revised manuscript. Of course, the possibility exists that editors will reject manuscripts upon initial review, never sending them to reviewers. It is our hope that the foregoing advice will prevent rejection at initial review.

When reviewers offer conflicting feedback, the practice at the *Journal of The First-Year Experience & Students in Transition* is for the editor to offer the authors guidance on which reviewer's advice to follow and why. In all instances, authors are given the opportunity to either reject or accept the guidance of the reviewers, but they must describe what actions they took in regard to that advice and their rationale in a separate letter returned with the revised manuscript.

Submission Ethics

Submission guidelines of all academic journals require that authors vouch for the originality of their work and that the manuscript is not currently under review by any other publication. While the lengthy review and publication cycle of an academic journal can be frustrating, offering a manuscript to one journal at a time is compulsory. Authors will also need to guarantee to the editor that the copyright for the material is held by no other entity.

Other Dissemination Outlets

In some instances, the report of a research study lends itself to publication outside academic journals. These outlets may be useful at the beginning, during, or at the end of the research project. Publishing pieces of the research in other periodicals or presenting some aspects of the research at conferences can help researchers articulate what they hope to find, what they are finding, or pieces of what they have found. The prospect of writing for an academic journal or editing, co-authoring, or authoring a book is daunting to many beginning researchers so the following discussion will begin with suggestions for presenting research in fairly low-risk venues and then move to descriptions of more lengthy and time-consuming projects.

Wikis, Blogs, Listservs, and Other Professional Networking Sites

One of the lowest risk approaches to publishing pieces of research is online at professional networking sites, including organization or association listservs and special interest wikis and blogs. Because the names and locations of these networks are ever-evolving and these spaces are not always formal outlets for publication, specific addresses for these sites will not be offered here. Researchers are increasingly finding that these venues offer important opportunities to ask questions about an ongoing research agenda or vet ideas emerging from the research. While posting on these sites may not necessarily be publishing in the traditional sense, it does allow the researcher to begin to fulfill the final promise of conducting studies—making them public.

As with the literature review, it is suggested that the researcher use the CRAAP (**C**urrency, **R**elevance, **A**uthority, **A**ccuracy, and **P**urpose) test to determine the quality of the network when considering joining. More information on this checklist, developed by librarians at Meriam Library at California State University, Chico can be found in Appendix A.

Conference Presentations

A researcher could spend nearly every week on the road presenting at professional gatherings listed in *The Chronicle of Higher Education*. The state, regional, and national arms of the American Educational Research Association alone could keep researchers quite busy submitting and presenting their studies. We recommend submitting and presenting research to a professional gathering at least once during a research project. Descriptions of typical presentation types are offered below.

Poster sessions. Many gatherings of individuals interested in scholarship on students in transition will offer the researcher opportunities to design and present posters of their research. Academic posters are typically created to present a synthesized version of the research report, including an introduction, brief rationale, a few citations of previous research most important to the study, data collection methods, findings or analysis, and conclusion. These sessions generally allow for an hour or more of informal interaction with a high percentage of the overall event attendee pool. The poster session hosts, usually one or more members of the research team, make brief remarks and answer questions about their research and may provide handouts. Poster sessions are typically held in large venues where numerous sessions are held concurrently, and where the participants move from one poster to the next. Researchers selected to present poster sessions have demonstrated at least a fair level of expertise in the field and have written a proposal that indicates the research is appropriate to the topic of the gathering, original, and based on sound research design and analysis, as well as offers reasonable conclusions. A poster session might be the ideal setting for researchers who have completed their studies and are in the process of writing a manuscript, either as a dissertation or for an academic journal. Synthesizing research to fit on two or three poster boards and within a five-minute talk is an excellent method for clarifying exactly what the study is about and what it may contribute to scholarship and practice.

Concurrent sessions. Across academic disciplines and educational organizations, the format for these sessions varies widely; therefore, criteria for submitting a proposal to present such a session should be thoroughly read and followed to the letter. Most conferences that traditionally hold concurrent sessions on research related to students in transition allocate two thirds of the time (typically an hour to 75 minutes) to a formal presentation and one third of the time to informal discussion. Presenting research in this manner is useful after a project is completed, as it allows for a rich discussion with a group of colleagues about methods, findings, and conclusions. Selection criteria for a research-based concurrent session are similar to that for a poster session with one notable exception. Concurrent sessions are typically reserved for presentations of research that are predicted to have broader appeal to the gathering's participants either because of the expertise of the researcher or the significance or scope of the study. Well-known researchers, multi-institutional research projects, and a groundbreaking subfield of inquiry are examples of typical draws for concurrent sessions.

Panel discussions. These multiperson presentations allow researchers to describe their projects, either in whole or in part, in the company of others who have conducted studies on similar topics or have used similar methods. The session is usually moderated by a person on, or off, the panel and time for the formal portion of each presentation is usually held to a minimum. The moderator may provide one or a few common questions about the research to the panelists beforehand, which shapes each panelist's discussion. Time is allotted either during or after the panel has concluded its remarks for the panelists and audience to interact around the shared topic of interest. The moderator may synthesize the discussion or provide closing remarks. Participants in a panel discussion are often invited by the gathering's organizers, who shape the panel around levels of expertise, types of research, findings, institution types, or other criteria. Panels may also be formed by one researcher asking colleagues from other campuses to serve as panelists because of the unique contributions they could make to a particular discussion. Once the panel is formed, a proposal seeking inclusion in a gathering is submitted for consideration to the organizing group.

Roundtable discussions. At academic gatherings, roundtable discussions are reserved for open discussion around an important issue or theme. Rather than make a formal presentation, session facilitators encourage and maintain substantive discussion. For the researcher, convening a roundtable may allow them to share emerging ideas related to their research project and learn from others' experiences around a topic of shared interest. Roundtables are the face-to-face equivalent of the online professional network. Convening a roundtable has at least one major pitfall for researchers. Because they so often are engrossed in their own project, it may be difficult to step back and share equal airtime with others. A researcher proposing a roundtable discussion should do so only at a point in the research when listening to colleagues would be of greatest benefit.

Academic Periodicals, Magazines, and Newsletters

At this point in the discussion, the reader should be able to predict the first advice we will give regarding submitting research to academic periodicals, magazines, or newsletters. That is, once he or she has identified avenues to pursue, obtain submission guidelines. Publications such as *Change, Liberal Education, About Campus, Academic Leader,* and *E-Source for College Transitions* are editor, not peer or blind, reviewed. The editors are selected for their expertise in a particular field and make determinations about what will appear in the publication, sometimes in consultation with associate or assistant editors or editorial boards.

The writing requirements for academic periodicals vary widely in solicitation strategies, length of manuscripts accepted, the amount of guidance and editing each manuscript receives, and so on. The language is always less formal than that found in an academic journal, and the components of a research journal article are rarely found in these types of publications. Typically, the readership is much larger and more diverse compared to an academic journal and is likely to include new professionals; classroom faculty; student affairs educators; policy makers; administrators; and, on occasion, constituents outside of higher education. Knowing the specific interest of the diverse audiences for these publications is critical. While writing to such a broad audience may, at first, be intimidating, being allowed the freedom to write outside academic journal conventions about salient parts of a research project can be a joy.

The responsibility researchers have to make their findings public should include engaging as many, and as wide a variety of individuals, as they can. In academic periodicals, the researchers are able to foresee, for example, the implications their research has on educational policy and practice. They may be allowed to editorialize or speculate from their findings in ways that are not possible in an academic journal. *About Campus,* for example, uses *The New Yorker* or *Harper's* to pattern its literary style. Not everyone in the academy can immediately write in that style. However, most editors of these publications are eager to share ideas about how to shape a manuscript for submission and are interested in including a wide spectrum of new, midlevel, and experienced writers on their pages.

Monographs and Books

Researchers who have generated enough high-quality material to appeal to a monograph or book-sized audience may consider submitting a proposal to an academic publisher. Monographs are multi-chapter volumes published in a series, such as Jossey-Bass' New Directions Series or the Research Reports on College Transitions offered by the National Resource Center for The First-Year Experience and Students in Transition. The Research Reports series publishes descriptions of original research of national significance that require more expansive treatment than the typical journal article. These monographs or books may contain the report of a single, large-scale study or may offer a collection of smaller research reports on a similar topic or research question (e.g., institutional research reports on outcomes related to first-year seminars). In addition to a presentation of research findings, these publications typically contain a review of the literature, which situates the current study in the context of the existing literature and research, and a discussion of the implications of the results on student learning, success, and institutional practice.

Researchers with an interest in turning their research project into a book are offered the same advice given throughout this chapter—obtain and follow to the letter the author's guidelines. Academic publishers who exhibit at most national higher education gatherings where researchers are present will invite proposals from individuals interested in using their research project as the seedbed for a book-length discussion. One good example of this type of book is *Student Success in College: Creating Conditions That Matter* (Kuh et al., 2005). This volume emerged from the Documenting Effective Educational Practice (DEEP) research project from the Center for Postsecondary Research at Indiana University. Even as a new scholar begins his or her very first research project, there is no harm in imagining how that project might be turned into at least one book.

Conclusion

This chapter's primary advice has regarded the importance of following publishing and submission guidelines and finding multiple opportunities to present research findings. The beginning sections were devoted to understanding the first, critical audience of a research manuscript submitted to an academic journal—the reviewer. If the researcher is able to work toward satisfying the reviewers, he or she is well on the way to successfully publishing in an academic journal. Alternative venues for making research available to other scholars and practitioners outside one's own campus were also proposed. Online networks are becoming increasingly important outlets for discussing or even publishing parts and processes of research projects and can also allow frustrated or exhilarated researchers to share their sorrows and triumphs. Face-to-face gatherings at state, regional, or national meetings or conferences offer several different session types for researchers to share all or part of their work. Presenting at a conference on research in progress can be highly motivating and an opportunity to network with other researchers, as well as provide reassurance that there are others sharing similar research experiences. Discussion of high-threshold projects (i.e., monographs and books) finished the chapter. From conception to publication, these often-daunting undertakings may stretch into years. If scholars have committed to completing a high-quality research project on students in transition, they likely have the passion and perseverance to complete publishing feats like these that may now seem far out of reach.

As the number of individuals interested in conducting and publishing research on students in transition steadily climbs and as the body of research on this topic grows, we are confident that the array of venues for publishing research in this field will also expand. Committed researchers will have multiple opportunities throughout their careers to make good on a most important promise that was noted at the beginning of this chapter, to share their research findings with other scholars and practitioners dedicated to the support and success of students in transition.

APPENDIX A

Additional Resources

APA Authors and Reviewers Resource site
www.apa.org/pubs/authors/index.aspx

CRAAP (Currency, Relevance, Authority, Accuracy, and Purpose) Test
www.csuchico.edu/lins/handouts/evalsites.html

E-Source for College Transitions
http://www.sc.edu/fye/esource

Journal of The First-Year Experience & Students in Transition author guidelines
www.sc.edu/fye/journal/submission.htm

Journal of The First-Year Experience & Students in Transition indices
www.sc.edu/fye/journal/journalindex.htm

National Resource Center for The First-Year Experience and Students in Transition website
www.sc.edu/fye

Appendix B

*Journal of The First-Year Experience &
Students in Transition*

Manuscript Review Form

Manuscript Title: _____

Reviewer: _____

Date Sent: _____

Please return this review form to: NRCJour@mailbox.sc.edu

	Weak	Acceptable	Strong	Comments
Overall Evaluation				
Evidence of new findings or ideas				
Potential contribution to the study of college student transitions				
Evidence of a compelling rationale for the research study				
Clarity of writing				
Currency and relevance of citations				
Appropriateness and clarity of tables and graphs				
Evidence of grounding in relevant theory or concepts				

	Weak	Acceptable	Strong	Comments
Usefulness of recommendations for practice and future research				
General Organization				
Accuracy of title				
Accuracy of abstract				
Presence and development of standard components of social science research article				
Methodology Review				
Clarity of hypotheses and research questions				
Adequate descriptions of sample and/or sampling methods				
Clarity of descriptions of measures and treatment procedures				
Appropriateness of research design for the study's hypotheses or research questions				
Appropriateness of statistical tests OR qualitative analyses used				
Clarity of presentation of findings				
Congruence of discussion/ recommendation section with the results				
Results situated in the context of previous studies/ professional literature				

Recommendations

_____ Accept

_____ Accept pending revisions (suggested revisions on separate page)

_____ Revise (see suggestions)

_____ Reject

Narrative Evaluation

Please comment on the strengths and weaknesses of the manuscript. Specifically address any items rated *weak*. Please make your comments for revision as specific as possible to help guide the authors' work. There is no need to mark the manuscript itself. All reviews and a synthesis by the journal editor will be forwarded to the authors. Thank you very much for your contributions as a member of the journal review board.

REFERENCES

Allison, P. D. (2001). *Missing data* (University Paper Series on Quantitative Applications in the Social Sciences, 136). Newbury Park, CA: Sage.

American Psychological Association (APA). (2005). *Concise rules of APA style*. Washington, DC: Author.

American Psychological Association (APA). (2009). *Publication manual of the American Psychological Association* (6th ed.). Washington, DC: Author.

Andrade, M. S. (2005). International students and the first year of college. *Journal of The First-Year Experience and Students in Transition, 17*(1), 101-129.

Astin, A. (1991). *Assessment for excellence: The philosophy and practice of assessment and evaluation in higher education*. Washington, DC: American Council on Education/Macmillan.

Aud, S., Hussar, W., Kena, G., Bianco, K., Frohlich, L., Kemp, J., Tahan, K. (2011). *The condition of Education 2011* (NCES 2011-033). U.S. Department of Education, National Center for Education Statistics. Washington, DC: U.S. Government Printing Office.

Auerbach, C. F., & Silverstein, L. B. (2003). *Qualitative data: An introduction to coding and analysis*. New York, NY: New York University.

Barefoot, B. O., Gardner, J. N., Cutright, M., Morris, L. V., Schroeder, C. C., Schwartz, S. W., Siegel, M. J., & Swing, R. J. (2005). *Achieving and sustaining institutional excellence for the first year of college*. San Francisco, CA: Jossey-Bass.

Baxter Magolda, M. B. (2009). The activity of meaning making: A holistic perspective on college student development. *Journal of College Student Development, 50*(6), 621-639.

Benjamin, D. P. (1993). A focus on American Indian college persistence. *Journal of American Indian College Persistence, 32*(2), 24-40.

Black, K. A., & Voelker, J. C. (2008). The role of preceptors in first-year student engagement in introductory courses. *Journal of The First-Year Experience & Students in Transition, 20*(2), 25-43.

Blackhurst, A. E., Akey, L. D., & Bobilya, A. J. (2003). A qualitative investigation of student outcomes in a residential learning community. *Journal of The First-Year Experience & Students in Transition, 15*(2), 35-59.

Bloor, M., Frankland, J., Thomas, M., & Robson, K. (2001). *Focus groups in social research.* London, UK: Sage.

Bogdan, R. C., & Biklen, S. K. (1998). *Qualitative research in education: An introduction to theory and methods* (3rd ed.). Needham Heights, MA: Allyn & Bacon.

Booth, W. C., Colomb, G. G., & Williams, J. M. (1995). *The craft of research.* Chicago, IL: University of Chicago.

Bordens, K. S., & Abbott, B. B. (1991). *Research design and methods.* London, UK: Mayfield.

Bowman, N. A. (2010). Can first-year college students accurately report their learning and development? *American Educational Research Journal, 47,* 466-496.

Brady, P., & Allingham, P. (2007). Help or hindrance? The role of secondary schools in a successful transition to university. *Journal of The First-Year Experience & Students in Transition, 19*(2), 47-67.

Bridges, W. (1980). *Transitions: Making sense of life's changes: Strategies for coping with the difficult, painful, and confusing times in your life.* Reading, MA: Addison-Wesley.

Brower, A. M. (1990). Student perceptions of life task demands as a mediator in the freshman year experience. *Journal of The Freshman Year Experience, 2*(2), 7-30.

Brower, A. M. (1994). Measuring student performances and performance appraisals with the College Life Task Assessment instrument. *Journal of The Freshman Year Experience, 6*(2), 7-36.

Brower, A. M. (1997). Prototype matching and striving for future-selves: Information management strategies in the transition to college. *Journal of The Freshman Year Experience & Students in Transition, 9*(1), 7-42.

Bryson, S., Smith, R., & Vineyard, G. (2002). Relationship of race, academic, and nonacademic information in predicting the first-year success of selected admissions first-year students. *Journal of The First-Year Experience & Students in Transition, 14*(1), 65-80.

Chaskes, J. (1996). The first-year student as immigrant. *Journal of The Freshman Year Experience & Students in Transition, 8*(1), 79-91.

Christie, N. G., & Dinham, S. M. (1991). Institutional and external influences on social integration in the freshman year. *Journal of Higher Education, 62*(4), 412-436.

Creswell, J. W. (2009). *Research design: Quantitative, qualitative, and mixed methods approaches* (3rd ed.). Thousand Oaks, CA: Sage.

Crissman Ishler, J. L. (2005). Today's first-year students. In M. L. Upcraft, J. N. Gardner, B. O. Barefoot, & Associates, *Challenging and supporting the first-year student* (pp. 15-26). San Francisco, CA: Jossey-Bass.

Croninger, R. G., & Douglas, K. M. (2005). Missing data and institutional research. In P. D. Umbach (Ed.), *Survey research emerging issues* (New Directions for Institutional Research, No. 127, pp. 33-50). San Francisco, CA: Jossey-Bass.

Coughlin, M. A. (2005). *Applications of intermediate/advanced statistics in institutional research.* Tallahassee, FL: Association for Institutional Research.

De Leeuw, E. D., Hox, J. J., & Dillman, D. A. (2008). *International handbook of survey methodology.* New York, NY: Lawrence Erlbaum Associates, Taylor & Francis Group.

Denzin, N. K., & Lincoln, Y. S. (Eds.). (2005). *The Sage handbook of qualitative research* (3rd ed.). Thousand Oaks, CA: Sage.

Durkheim, E. (1951). Suicide: A study in sociology. New York, NY: The Free Press.

Earl, W. R. (1988). Intrusive advising of freshmen in academic difficulty, *NACADA Journal, 8*, 27-33.

Erickson, L. E., Peters, C. B., & Strommer, D. W. (2006). *Teaching first-year college students.* San Francisco, CA: Jossey-Bass.

Fidler, D. S., & Henscheid, J. M. (2001). *Primer for research on the college student experience.* Columbia, SC: University of South Carolina, National Resource Center for The First-Year Experience and Students in Transition.

Fidler, D. S., & Hoover, D. R. (1991, Fall). Call for research: National Resource Center for The Freshman Year Experience suggests research designs to investigate possible biases from volunteers and non-volunteers in freshman studies. *The Freshman Year Experience Newsletter*, 10-11.

Fidler, P. P., Neururer-Rotholz, J., & Richardson, S. (1999). Teaching the freshman seminar: Its effectiveness in promoting faculty development. *Journal of The First-Year Experience & Students in Transition, 11*(2), 59-74.

Fowler, F. J., Jr. (1995). *Improving survey questions: Design and evaluation* (Applied Social Research Methods Series, vol. 38). Thousand Oaks, CA: Sage.

Franklin, K. K. (2000). Shared and connected learning in a freshman learning community. *Journal of The First-Year Experience & Students in Transition, 12*(2), 33-60.

Fratrantuono, M. J., & Senecal, K. S. (1996). Matching methods to objectives and assessing results: A simulation in a freshman seminar about international relations. *Journal of The Freshman Year Experience & Students in Transition, 8*(2), 57-78.

Friday, R. A. (1989). Training freshman seminar faculty. *Journal of The Freshman Year Experience, 1*(2), 59-82.

Friday, R. A. (1990). Faculty training: From group process to collaborative learning. *Journal of The Freshman Year Experience, 2*(1), 49-67.

Friedman, D., & Marsh, E. G. (2009). What type of first-year seminar is most effective? A comparison of thematic seminars and college transition/success seminars. *Journal of The First-Year Experience & Students in Transition, 21*(1), 29-42.

Fuertes, J. N., Sedlacek, W. E., Roger, P. R., & Mohr, J. J. (2000). Correlates of universal-diverse orientation among first-year university students. *Journal of The First-Year Experience & Students in Transition, 12*(1), 45-59.

Gall, M. D., Borg, W. R., & Gall, J. P. (1996). *Educational research: An introduction* (6th ed.). New York, NY: Longman.

Gardner, J. N., Barefoot, B. O., & Swing, R. L. (2001a). *Guidelines for evaluating the first-year experience at two-year colleges* (2nd ed.). Columbia, SC: University of South Carolina, National Resource Center for The First-Year Experience and Students in Transition.

Gardner, J. N., Barefoot, B. O., & Swing, R. L. (2001b). *Guidelines for evaluating the first-year experience at four-year colleges* (2nd ed.). Columbia, SC: University of South Carolina, National Resource Center for The First-Year Experience and Students in Transition.

Glaser, B. G. (1978). *Theoretical sensitivity: Advances in the methodology of grounded theory*. Mill Valley, CA: The Sociology Press.

Gordon, V. (1991). The evolution of a freshman seminar course: A case study. *Journal of The Freshman Year Experience, 3*(2), 107-116.

Grant, L., & Fine, G. A. (1992). Sociology unleashed: Creative directions in classical ethnography. In M. D. LeCompte, W. L. Millroy, & J. Preissle (Eds.), *The handbook of qualitative research in education* (pp. 405-446). San Diego, CA: Academic Press.

Guba, E. G., & Lincoln, Y. S. (2005). Paradigmatic controversies, contradictions, and emerging influences. In N. K. Denzin & Y. S. Lincoln (Eds.), *The Sage handbook of qualitative research* (3rd ed., pp. 191-215). Thousand Oaks, CA: Sage.

Hammersley, M., & Atkinson. P. (1983). *Ethnography: Principles in practice.* London, UK: Tavistock.

Harmon, B. V. (2006). A qualitative study of the learning processes and outcomes associated with students who serve as peer mentors. *Journal of The First-Year Experience & Students in Transition, 18*(2), 53-82.

Harmon, W. W., & Rhatigan, J. J. (1990). Academic course for parents of first-year students impacts favorably on student retention. *Journal of The Freshman Year Experience, 2*(1), 85-95.

Henscheid, J. M. (1996). *Residential learning communities and the freshman year.* Unpublished doctoral dissertation, Washington State University, Pullman.

Heron, J., & Reason, P. (1997). A participatory inquiry paradigm. *Qualitative Inquiry, 3*(3), 274-294.

Hinni, J., & Eison, J. (1990). Helping freshman parents see the value of general education courses. *Journal of The Freshman Year Experience, 2*(2), 89-99.

Hofer, B. K. (2008). The electronic tether: Parental regulation, self-regulation, and the role of technology in college transitions. *Journal of The First-Year Experience & Students in Transition, 20*(2), 9-24.

Hoover, D. R. (1991). Guidelines for conducting college persistence/education research. *Journal of The Freshman Year Experience, 3*(1), 71-84.

Hossler, D. (Ed.) 1991. *Evaluating student recruitment and retention programs.* San Francisco, CA: Jossey-Bass.

Iaccino, J. F. (1989). Evaluation of Illinois Benedictine's freshman advising program. *Journal of The Freshman Year Experience, 1*(1), 45-52.

Jaeger, R. M. (1993). *Statistics: A spectator sport* (2nd ed.). Newbury Park, CA: Sage.

Johnson, B., & Christensen, L. (2008). *Educational research: Quantitative, qualitative, and mixed methods* (3rd ed.). Thousand Oaks, CA: Sage.

Johnson, V. K., Kerr, S., Gans, S. E., & Bierschwale, D. (2009). Adjustment to college before and after September 11, 2001. *Journal of The First-Year Experience & Students in Transition, 21*(1), 93-112.

Jones, S. R. (2002). (Re)writing the word: Methodological strategies and issues in qualitative research. *Journal of College Student Development, 43*(4), 461-473.

Jones, R. S., Torres, V., & Arminio, J. (2006). *Negotiating the complexities of qualitative research in higher education: Fundamental elements and issues.* New York, NY: Taylor and Francis.

Ketkar, K., & Bennett, S. (1989). Strategies for evaluating a freshman studies program. *Journal of The Freshman Year Experience, 1*(1), 33-44.

Keyton, J. (2006). *Communication research: Asking questions, finding answers* (2nd ed.). New York, NY: McGraw-Hill.

Kim, E. (2009). Navigating college life: The role of peer networks in first-year college adaptation experience of minority immigrant students. *Journal of The First-Year Experience & Students in Transition, 21*(2), 9-34.

Kinzie, J., & Kuh, G. (2004). Going DEEP: Learning from campuses that share responsibility for student success. *About Campus, 9*(5), 2-8.

Kirk-Kuwaye, C., & Kirk-Kuwaye, M. (2007) A study of engagement patterns of lateral and vertical transfer students during their first semester at a public research university. *Journal of The First-Year Experience and Students in Transition, 19*(2), 9-27.

Koch, A. K., Foote, S. M., Hinkle, S. E., Keup, J., & Pistilli, M. D. (Eds). (2007). *The first-year experience in American higher education: An annotated bibliography* (4th ed.). Columbia, SC: University of South Carolina, National Resource Center for The First-Year Experience and Students in Transition.

Krause, K. D. (2007). Social involvement and commuter students: The first-year student voice. *Journal of The First-Year Experience & Students in Transition, 19*(1), 27-45.

Krueger, R. A. (1998). *Moderating focus groups.* Thousand Oaks, CA: Sage.

Kuh, G. D., Schuh, J., Whitt, E., & Associates. (1991). *Involving colleges.* San Francisco, CA: Jossey-Bass.

Kuh, G. D., Kinzie, J., Schuh, J. H., Whitt, E. J., & Associates. (2005). *Student success in college: Creating conditions that matter.* San Francisco, CA: Jossey-Bass.

Kuh, G. D., Kinzie, J., Schuh, J. H., Whitt, E. J., & Associates. (2010). *Student success in college: Creating conditions that matter.* San Francisco, CA: Jossey-Bass.

LeCompte, M. D., Millroy, W. L., & Preissle, J. (Eds.). (1992). *The handbook of qualitative research in education.* San Diego, CA: Academic Press.

Liljequist, L., & Stone, S. (2009). Measuring the success of a summer reading program: A five-year study. *Journal of The First-Year Experience & Students in Transition, 21*(2), 87-105.

Magolda, P. (1997). New student disorientation: Becoming a member of an academic community. *Journal of The Freshman Year Experience & Students in Transition, 9*(1), 43-104.

Maxwell, J. A. (1996). *Qualitative research design: An interactive approach* (Applied Social Research Methods Series, Vol. 41). Thousand Oaks, CA: Sage.

McBroom, E., Fife, E. M., & Nelson, C. L. (2008). Risky business: The college transition, loneliness, and alcohol consumption. *Journal of The First-Year Experience & Students in Transition, 20*(2), 45-64.

McClure, A. I., Atkinson, M. P., & Wills, J. B. (2008). Transferring teaching skills: Faculty development effects from a first-year inquiry program. *Journal of The First-Year Experience & Students in Transition, 20*(1), 31-52.

McGillin, V.A. (2003). Research versus assessment: What's the difference? *Academic Advising Today, 26*(4). Retrieved from http://www.nacada.ksu.edu/AAT/NW26_4.htm

Merriam, S. B., & Simpson, E. L. (2000). *A guide to research for educators and trainers of adults* (2nd ed.). Malabar, FL: Krieger.

Miles, M. B., & Huberman, A. M. (1994). *Qualitative data analysis: An expanded sourcebook* (2nd ed.). Thousand Oaks, CA: Sage.

Mills, M. T. (2010). Tools of engagement: Success course influence on student engagement. *Journal of The First-Year Experience & Students in Transition, 22*(2), 9-22.

Miller, J. W., Janz, J. C., & Chen, C. (2007). The retention impact of a first-year seminar on students with varying pre-college academic performance. *Journal of The First-Year Experience & Students in Transition, 19*(1), 47-62.

Milville, M. L., & Sedlacek, W. (1994). Attitudes of freshmen toward Arab-Americans: A university campus dilemma. *Journal of The Freshman Year Experience, 6*(2), 77-88.

Moffatt, M. (1989). *Coming of age in New Jersey: College and American culture*. New Brunswick, NJ: Rutgers.

Morgan, D. L. (1997). *Focus groups as qualitative research* (2nd ed., Qualitative Research Methods Series, No. 16). London, UK: Sage.

Nicol, A. A. M., & Pexman, P. M. (2010). *Presenting your findings: A practical guide for creating tables* (6th ed.) Washington, DC: American Psychological Association.

Nathan, R. (2005). *My freshman year: What a professor learned by becoming a student*. Ithaca, NY: Cornell University.

Noledon, D. F., & Sedlacek, W. E. (1996). Race differences in attitudes, skills, and behaviors among academically talented students. *Journal of The Freshman Year Experience & Students in Transition, 8*(2), 43-56.

Pace, C. R. (1979). *Measuring outcomes of college: Fifty years of findings and recommendations for the future*. San Francisco, CA: Jossey-Bass.

Padgett, R. D., & Keup, J. R. (in press). *2009 National Survey of First-Year Seminars: Ongoing efforts to support students in transition*. Columbia, SC: University of South Carolina, National Resource Center for The First-Year Experience and Students in Transition.

Pascarella, E. T., & Terenzini, P. T. (2005). *How college affects students: A third decade of research*. San Francisco, CA: Jossey-Bass.

Rea, L. M., & Parker, R. A. (1997). *Designing and conducting survey research: A comprehensive guide*. San Francisco, CA: Jossey-Bass.

Rice, R. (1992). Reactions of participants to either one-week pre-college orientation or to freshman seminar courses. *Journal of The Freshman Year Experience, 4*(2), 85-100.

Richardson, S. M., & Sullivan, M. M. (1994). Identifying noncognitive factors that influence success of academically underprepared freshmen. *Journal of The First-Year Experience & Students in Transition, 6*(2), 89-100.

Robinson, W. S. (1951).The logical structure of analytical induction. *American Sociological Review, 16*, 812-818.

Roderick, C., & Carusetta, E. (2006). Experiencing first-year university in a problem-based learning context. *Journal of The First-Year Experience & Students in Transition, 18*(1), 9-27.

Schwitzer, A. M., Ancis, J. R., & Griffin, O. T. (1998). Validating a proposed model of African-American students' social adjustment. *Journal of The First-Year Experience & Students in Transition, 11*(1), 77-102.

Seldin, P. (1990). *How administrators can improve teaching.* San Francisco, CA: Jossey-Bass.

Smith, D. N., Goldfine, R., & Windham, M. (2009). Comparing student learning outcomes in an independent section of a first-year seminar to a first-year seminar embedded in a learning community. *Journal of The First-Year Experience & Students in Transition, 21*(2), 47-64.

Smith, B. L., MacGregor, J., Matthews, R., & Gabelnick, F. (2004). *Learning communities: Reforming undergraduate education.* San Francisco, CA: Jossey-Bass.

Starke, M. C., Harth, M., & Sirianni, F. (2001). Retention, bonding, and academic achievement: Success of a first-year seminar. *Journal of The First-Year Experience & Students in Transition, 13*(2), 7-36.

Stewart, T. (2009). Service-learning and honors undergraduates: The effect on social dominance orientation. *Journal of The First-Year Experience & Students in Transition, 21*(2), 65-86.

Strauss, A. L. (1987). *Qualitative analysis for social scientists.* Cambridge, UK: Cambridge University.

Strauss, A., & Corbin, J. (1998). *Basics of qualitative research: Techniques and procedures for developing grounded theory.* Thousand Oaks, CA: Sage.

Strayhorn, T. L. (2009). An examination of the impact of first-year seminars on correlates of college student retention. *Journal of The First-Year Experience & Students in Transition, 21*(1), 9-27.

Suskie, L. A. (Ed.) (1996). *Questionnaire survey research: What works?* (2nd ed.). Tallahassee, FL: Association for Institutional Research.

Swing, R. L. (2004). What's so special about assessment in the first year of college? *Assessment Update, 16(2),* 1-4.

Thomas, S. L., Heck, R. H., & Bauer, K. W. (2005). Weighting and adjusting for design effects in secondary data analyses. In P. D. Umbach (Ed.), *Survey research emerging issues* (New Directions for Institutional Research, no. 127, pp. 51-72). San Francisco, CA: Jossey-Bass.

Terenzini, P. T., Pascarella, E. T., & Blimling, G. S. (1996). Students' out-of-class experiences and their influence on learning and cognitive development: A literature review. *Journal of College Student Development, 37*(2), 149-162.

Tieu, T.-T., & Prancer, S. M. (2009). Cocurricular involvement and first-year students' transition to university: Quality vs. quantity of involvement. *Journal of The First-Year Experience & Students in Transition, 21*(1), 43-64.

Tinto, V. (1987). *Leaving college: Rethinking the causes and cures of student attrition*. Chicago, IL: University of Chicago.

Tinto, V. (1994). *Leaving college: Rethinking the causes and cures of student attrition* (2nd ed.). Chicago, IL: University of Chicago.

Tinto, V., & Goodsell, A. (1994). Freshman interest groups and the first-year experience: Constructing student communities in a large university. *Journal of The Freshman Year Experience & Students in Transition, 6*(1), 7-28.

Tobolowsky, B. F. (2005). *The 2003 National Survey of First-Year Seminars: Continuing innovations in the collegiate curriculum*. Columbia, SC: University of South Carolina, National Resource Center for The First-Year Experience and Students in Transition.

Tobolowsky, B. F., & Associates. (2008). *2006 National Survey of First-Year Seminars: Continuing innovations in the college curriculum* (Monograph No. 51). Columbia, SC: University of South Carolina, National Resource Center for The First-Year Experience and Students in Transition.

Tobolowsky, B. F., & Cox, B. E. (Eds.). (2007). *Shedding light on sophomores: An exploration of the second college year* (Monograph No. \47). Columbia, SC: University of South Carolina, National Resource Center for The First-Year Experience and Students in Transition.

Tobolowsky, B. F., Cox, B. E., & Wagner, M. T. (2005). *Exploring the evidence, Volume III: Reporting research on first-year seminars* (Monograph No. 42). Columbia, SC: University of South Carolina, National Resource Center for The First-Year Experience and Students in Transition.

Troxel, W. G., & Cutright, M. (Eds.). (2008). *Exploring the evidence: Initiatives in the first college year* (Monograph No. 49). Columbia, SC: University of South Carolina, National Resource Center for The First-Year Experience & Students in Transition.

Tukuno, K. A. (Ed.). (2008). *Graduate students in transition: Assisting students through the first year* (Monograph No. 50). Columbia, SC: University of South Carolina, National Resource Center for The First-Year Experience and Students in Transition.

Upcraft, M. L., Gardner, J. N., & Barefoot, B. O. (Eds.). (2005). *Challenging and supporting the first-year student: A handbook for improving the first year of college*. San Francisco, CA: Jossey-Bass.

Volkwein, J. F., & Yin, A. C. (2010). Measurement issues in assessment. In J. F. Volkwein (Ed.), *Assessing student outcomes* (New Directions for Institutional Research, No. S1, pp. 141-154). San Francisco, CA: Jossey-Bass.

Walpole, M., Simmerman, H., Mack, C., Mills, J. T., Scales, M., & Albano, D. (2008). Bridge to success: Insight into summer bridge program students' college transition. *Journal of The First-Year Experience & Students in Transition, 20*(1), 11-30.

Weissman, J., & Magill, B. A. (2008). Developing a student typology to examine the effectiveness of first-year seminars. *Journal of The First-Year Experience & Students in Transition, 20*(2), 65-90.

Western Interstate Commission for Higher Education. (2008). *Knocking at the college door: Projections of high school graduates by state and race/ethnicity 1992-2022.* Boulder, CO: Author.

Windschitl, M., & Leshem-Ackerman, A. (1997). Learning teams students and the college e-mail culture. *Journal of The Freshman Year Experience & Students in Transition, 9*(2), 53-82.

Wolcott, H. F. (1995). *The art of fieldwork.* Walnut Creek, CA: AltaMira.

Wolf-Wendel, L. E., Tuttle, K., & Keller-Wolff, C. M. (1999). Assessment of a freshman summer transition program in an open-admissions institution. *Journal of The First-Year Experience & Students in Transition, 11*(2), 7-32.

INDEX

A

About Campus, 14, 100
abstracting databases, 7
academic journals. See also academic periodicals; academic reviewers
    author's guidelines for, 86
    ethics of submitting to, 96
    manuscript style for, 86
    review form, 87
Academic Leader, 100
academic periodicals, 100
academic reviewers. See also academic journals
    on general organization of manuscripts, 92
    on methodological components, 92–95
    names and number of, 88
    overall evaluation by, 87–92
    post-review steps, 95–96
academically underprepared first-year students, 6
accountability movement, student data and, 72
action research, 50
African American students' social adjustment, 6
Akey, L. D., 55
Allingham, P., 30, 42
American Educational Research Association, 97
analysis of covariance (ANCOVA), 81
analysis of variance (ANOVA), 81, 82
analytic induction procedure, modified, 58
analytical abilities, of qualitative researcher, 44
Ancis, J. R., 6
Andrade, M. S., 42
APA Authors and Reviewers Resource site, 87, 103
APA Manual (*Publication Manual of the American Psychological Association*), 49, 86–87, 90, 95

Note: page numbers with italicized f indicate figures.

applied research, definition of, ix
Arminio, J., 20
assessment, research vs., ix–x, 91–92
Assessment Update, 14
association, measures of, 79–80
Astin, A., 15, 66
Attebury, R., 7
audience, for research, 32
Auerbach, C. F., 59
Australian Education Index, 8

B

Barefoot, B. O., x, 12
basic research, definition of, ix
Baxter Magolda, M. B., 32
Belmont Report, 34
beneficence, for human subjects, 34
Bennett, S., 15
bias in sample selection, limitation of, 74–75, 76–77
Bierschwale, D., 81–82
big picture vision, of quantitative researcher, 65
Biklen, S. K., 59
Black, K. A., 73–74
Blackhurst, A. E., 55
Blimling, G. S., 56
blogs, for publishing research results, 97
Bloor, M., 54
Bobilya, A. J., 55
Bogdan, R. C., 59
books
    literature reviews of, 7
    publishing research results in, 101
Booth, W. C., 2
Brady, P., 30
Bridges, William, 5
British Educational Research Journal, 16
Brower, A. M., 6, 56
budget for research, 49

C

Carusetta, E., 52

Center for Postsecondary Research at Indiana University, 32

central tendency measures, 79

Challenging and Supporting the First-Year Student, 12

Change, 14, 99

Chaskes, J., 56, 59

Chen, C., 70

chi-squared analysis, 82

Christensen, L., 3–4, 51, 90

Chronicle of Higher Education, The, 10, 97

Claremont Graduate University, The, 10

closed-end interviews, 53–54

codes, qualitative research, 59

collaborative approach, to qualitative research, 47, 50

College Senior Survey (CSS), 71

College Student Expectations Questionnaire (CSXQ) assessment, 71

College Student Experiences Questionnaire (CSEQ) assessment, 71

College Student Personnel Abstracts. See Higher Education Abstracts

College Teaching, 14

Colomb, G. G., 2

Coming of Age in New Jersey (Moffatt), 51

Community College Survey of Student Engagement (CCSSE), 28, 71

concept of journal article, 91

Concise Rules of APA Style, 86

conclusion drawing and verification, 57–58

concurrent sessions, at conferences, 98-99

conference presentations, of research results, 97–100

confirmatory research, 3

confounding variables, 75

constructivism, as approach to qualitative research, 47, 49

contextual literature, 12

control variables, 69

Cooperative Institutional Research Program's (CIRP)
    College Senior Survey (CSS), 71
    Freshman Survey, 31, 71, 81
    Your First College Year (YFCY) survey, x, 71

Corbin, J., 46

correlations, measures of, 80

Coughlin, M. A., 83

CRAAP (Currency, Relevance, Authority, Accuracy, and Purpose) test, 97, 103
Creswell, J. W., 22
critical theory, qualitative research and, 47, 49–50
cross-sectional research designs, 78
CSA Sociological Abstracts, 11

D

data analysis, in qualitative research, 57–59
data collection instrument/tool
   academic reviewers on, 93
   for quantitative research, 27–28, 72–73
data collection procedures
   analysis in the field, 53
   characteristics of, 51
   observations, 52
data display, 57
data reduction, 57
data sources, for quantitative research, 70–73
Database of Research in International Education, 8
databases, accessing and using, 7–11
decision tree analysis, 82
deductive research, 3–4, 25, 27
Denzin, N. K., 46
dependent variables, 68, 69–70
descriptive statistics, 79–81, 83–84
discriminant analysis, 82
discussion, reviewers on congruence of results, recommendations and, 94
dissertations, statement of purpose for, 66
Dissertations and Theses (database), 11
document analysis, in qualitative research, 56–57
Documenting Effective Educational Practice (DEEP) project, 4, 32, 101
Durkheim, E., 6

E

EBSCO Publishing, 9, 10
EdResearch Online, 8
Education Abstracts, 8
Education Full Text, 8
Education Index, 8

Education Index Retrospective (1929-1983), 9
Education Research Complete, 9
Education Resources Information Center (ERIC), 8, 9–10
Educational Abstracts. See Educational Administration Abstracts
Educational Action Research, 16
Educational Administration Abstracts, 9
Educational Administration Quarterly, 9
Educational and Psychological Measurement, 16
Educational Benchmarking Inc., x
Educational Leadership, 10
Educational Research, 16
Educational Research Abstracts (ERA) Online, 9
Educational Research Quarterly, 16
Educational Researcher, 16
Educational Technology Abstracts, 9–10
empathy, of qualitative researcher, 43
endings, in transitions, 5
equal-but-different measures, 82
E-Source for College Transitions, 13, 99, 103
ethics, 34, 47, 96
existing research, 33, 70–72
experimental research design, 27–28, 78
exploratory analysis, 71
exploratory research, 3
Exploring the Evidence, Volume III: Reporting Research on First-Year Seminars
(Tobolowsky, Cox, & Wagner), 13
Exploring the Evidence: Initiatives in the First College Year (Troxel & Cutright), 13

F
factor analysis, 82
Fidler, Dorothy S., 20, 91
Fidler, Paul P., 53, 91
field analysis, 53
Fife, E. M., 83
findings. See also manuscripts; research results
reviewers on display of, 94
reviewers on new or important, 88–89
Fine, G. A., 56
First-Year Experience in American Higher Education, The: An Annotated Bibliography
(Koch, Foote, Hinkle, Keup, & Pistilli), 13

first-year experience movement, age of, vii
First-Year Initiative (FYI) benchmarking survey, 71
first-year seminars, earliest examples of, vii
flexibility, of qualitative researcher, 44
focus groups, 54–55
Focus Groups as Qualitative Research (Morgan), 54
Focus Groups in Social Research (Bloor, Frankland, Thomas, and Robson), 54
framing the question. See also research question
    current theories on students in transition, 5–6
    interests, topics, questions, and problems, 2–3
    literature review for, 6–17
    role in theory of, 3–4
Frankland, J., 54
Franklin, K. K., 6
Fratrantuono, M. J., 56
frequency distributions, measures of, 79–80
Freshman Survey, Cooperative Institutional Research Program's (CIRP), 31, 71, 81
Freshman Year Experience Newsletter, The, 15
Friedman, D., 48
Fuertes, J. N., 6
full-text databases, 7

G
Gans, S. E., 81–82
Gardner, J. N., 12
Goodsell, A., 51
Gordon, V., 57
Graduate Students in Transition: Assisting Students Through the First Year (Tukuno), 13
Grant, L., 56
graphical data display, 57, 90, 94
Griffin, O. T., 6
group interviews, 54–55
Guba, E. G., 49, 50
Guidelines for Evaluating The First-Year Experience at Four-Year Colleges, 2nd Edition (Gardner, Barefoot, & Swing), 12
Guidelines for Evaluating The First-Year Experience at Two-Year Colleges, 2nd Edition (Gardner, Barefoot, & Swing), 12

H

Harmon, B. V., 53–54
Henscheid, J. M., 20, 51
Heron, J., 49
hierarchical linear modeling, 82
Higher Education Abstracts, 10
Hispanic Outlook in Higher Education, The, 14
Hofer, B. K., 66
Hoover, D. R., 15
Hossler, D., 15
Huberman, A. M., 57, 59
human subjects, principles for using, 34
H.W. Wilson Company, 8
hypotheses
    dependent variable and primary independent variables and, 69–70
    in quantitative research, 27, 65–67
    write-up of, 92

I

Iaccino, J. F., 15
implications for practice, journal articles on, 91–92
important findings or ideas, reviewers on, 88–89
independent variables, 68–70
indexing databases, 7
Indiana University, Center for Postsecondary Research at, 32
inductive research, 3, 4, 22, 23–24, 36. See also analytic induction procedure, modified
inferential statistics, 81–84
Inputs-Environment-Outcomes model, 66
Institutional Review Boards (IRBs), 34
interest areas, for research, 2
International Journal of Qualitative Studies in Education, 16
International Journal of Research & Method in Education, 16
interviews
    in groups, 54–55
    in qualitative research, 24, 53–54
Issues in Educational Research, 16

J

Janz, J. C., 70
Johnson, B., 3–4, 51, 90
Johnson, V. K, 81–82
Jones, R. S., 20
Jossey-Bass' New Directions Series, 100
Journal of American Indian College Persistence, 14
Journal of Blacks in Higher Education, The, 14
Journal of College Orientation and Transition, The, 14
Journal of College Student Development, The, 14
Journal of College Student Retention, 14
Journal of Developmental Education, 14
Journal of Education, 10
Journal of Educational Administration, 9
Journal of Educational Measurement, 16
Journal of Higher Education, The, 10, 87
Journal of Mixed Methods Research, The, 16
Journal of The First-Year Experience & Students in Transition
    Article Review Form, 105–107
    author's guidelines for, 86
    descriptive statistics studies in, 80
    document and literature reviews in, 56
    reviewer feedback for, 96
    reviewers for, 88
    as substantive literature for research, 13
    types of research featured in, 6
    URL for journal and indices to, 103
    as vehicle for new research, vii
    verbs from research questions and purpose statements of studies published in,
        36, 36f
Journal of The Freshman Year Experience, 13
Journal of The Freshman Year Experience & Students in Transition, 13
justice, for human subjects, 34

K

Keller-Wolff, C. M., 54
Kerr, S., 81–82
Ketkar, K., 15
Kim, E., 24–25

Kirk-Kuwaye, C., 42
Kirk-Kuwaye, M., 42
Krause, K. D., 54–55
Krueger, R. A., 55
Kuh, G. D., 5

L

leadership, better-than-expected-student engagement and, 4
Learning and Study Strategies Inventory (LASSI), 71
LeCompte, M. D., 46
Leshem-Ackerman, A., 55
Liberal Education, 14, 99
life role complexity, 6
limited surveys, 55–56
Lincoln, Y. S., 46, 49, 51
listening skills, of qualitative researcher, 43
listservs, for publishing research results, 97
literature review
    about, 6–7
    of contextual literature, 12
    of methodological literature, 15–17
    for qualitative research, 24, 56–57
    of research databases, 7–11
    of substantive literature, 12–15
logistic regression, 82
longitudinal research designs, 78, 79

M

magazines, submitting research to, 99–100
Magill, B. A., 66, 82
Magolda, P., 52
manuscript title, 88
manuscripts
    academic reviewers on general organization of, 92
    after the review, 95–96
    APA style for, 95
    general organization review of, 92–95
    methodological components of, 92–95
    other dissemination outlets for, 96–101

overall evaluation by academic reviewers of, 87–92
submission ethics, 96
Marsh, E. G., 48
mathematical abilities, 64
McBroom, E., 83
means, measures of, 79
Measurement: Interdisciplinary Research and Perspectives, 16
measures. See data collection instrument/tool
Measuring Outcomes of College: Fifty Years of Findings and Recommendations for the Future (Pace), 1
medians, measures of, 79
mediating variables, 69
mentorship programs, earliest examples of, vii
Meriam Library at California State University, Chico, 97
meta-analyses, 24, 56–57
methodological literature, 15–17
methodology
    comparison of qualitative vs. quantitative research, 20, 22, 26*f*
    functional elements of, 31–33, 35
    methods compared with, 19–20
    mixed, 29–30
    myths about, 21*f*
    perspective of the researcher and, 37–38
    purpose of study, 35–36
    qualitative research, 22–25
    in qualitative research proposal, 45–46
    quantitative research, 25, 27–28
    selecting, 30–33, 35–38
methods
    definition and usage of, 19–20
    for qualitative research, 24
Miles, M. B., 57, 59
Miller, J. W., 70
Millroy, W. L., 46
Mills, M. T., 28
Milville, M. L., 55
mixed-methodology research, 29–30
modes, measures of, 79
Moffatt, M., 51
Mohr, J. J., 6
monographs, publishing research results in, 101

Morgan, D. L., 54
motivation-related noncognitive factors, 6
multivariate analyses, 82–83, 84
Multivariate Behavioral Research, 16
My Freshman Year: What a Professor Learned by Becoming a Student (Nathan), 51

N

Nathan, R., 51
National On-Campus Report, 14
National Resource Center for The First-Year Experience and Students in Transition
    on applied research, ix
    establishment of, vii
    National Survey of First-Year Seminars, 81
    Research Reports on College Transitions, 100–101
    substantive literature published by, 12–14
    website for, 103
National Survey of First-Year Seminars,13
National Survey of Student Engagement (NSSE)
    Annual Report of, 80
    DEEP project and, 4
    as national research project, x
    secondary data analysis from, 31, 71
National Teaching & Learning Forum, 14
Nelson, C. L., 83
Neururer-Rotholz, J., 53
neutral zone, in transitions, 5
new beginnings, in transitions, 5
new findings or ideas, reviewers on, 88
newsletters, submitting research to, 99–100
Noledon, D. F., 55
nonresponse bias, 75, 76
NSSE. See National Survey of Student Engagement

O

objectivity, of quantitative researcher, 64–65
observations, in qualitative research, 24, 51-52
open-ended interviews, 53–54
open-ended surveys, 24, 29
organizational skills, of qualitative researcher, 43–44

original data, for quantitative research, 70, 72–73

outcomes of interest, 22

P

Pace, R., 1

panel discussions, at conferences, 99

participants, research, 33, 73–77, 92–93

participatory approach, to qualitative research, 47, 50

partnerships between academic and student affairs personnel, 4

Pascarella, E. T., 56

path analysis, 82

patience, of qualitative researcher, 43

peer-reviewed journals, 49

Perceptions, Expectations, Emotions and Knowledge (PEEK) about College assessment tool, 71

perspective of the researcher, methodology and, 37–38

planfulness, of quantitative researcher, 64

population sampling, 75–76

positivism

    qualitative research and, 47, 49, 50

    quantitative research and, 37, 63

poster sessions, at conferences, 98

postpositivism

    qualitative research and, 47, 49, 50

    quantitative research and, 37, 63

power of one, better-than-expected-student engagement and, 4

Prancer, S. M., 66–67

Preissle, J., 46

pre-posttest design, 79

Presenting Your Findings (Nicol & Pexman), 86

previously collected data, 33, 70–72

primary data analysis, 31

print materials, 7

problem, for research. See also research question

    development of, 3

    literature review and, 6, 12

    observations and, 52

    in qualitative research, 45

    qualitative research report on, 61

Professional Development Collection, 10

professional networking sites, for publishing research results, 97
program evaluation, research vs., 91–92
PsychINFO, 11
Publication Manual of the American Psychological Association (APA Manual), 49, 86, 90, 95
publishing results. See research results
purpose of study
    dependent variable and primary independent variables and, 69–70
    methodology selection and, 35–36, 36*f*
    in qualitative research, 45
    in quantitative research, 65–67

Q

qualitative data analysis software, 48
qualitative research
    approaches to, 49–51
    characteristics of, 41–43
    data analysis, 57–59
    data collection procedures and types of data, 51–57
    definition and description of, 22–23
    example of, 24–25
    first-person voice in reporting on, 89–90
    generalizability, validity, and reliability in, 59–60
    individuals drawn to, 37–38
    methods for, 24
    myths about, 21*f*
    proposal for, 44–49
    quantitative research combined with, 29–30
    quantitative research compared with, 20, 22, 26*f*
    research question and purpose of, 35–36, 36f
    role and disposition of researcher conducting, 43–44
    role of theory in, 3–4
    writing the report on, 60–61
quantitative research
    characteristics of, 63–65
    clarifying purpose of, 65–67
    definition and description of, 25, 27
    definition and identification of variables, 67–70
    identifying sources of data and participants, 70–77
    individuals drawn to, 37–38

myths about, 21*f*
   qualitative research combined with, 29–30
   qualitative research compared with, 20, 22, 26*f*
   research design, 77–79
   research question and purpose of, 35–36, 36*f*
   role of theory in, 3–4
   statistical methods, 77, 79–84
   third-person voice in reporting on, 89
quasi-experimental research designs, 78
question. See framing the question; research question

R
random sampling, 75–76
rationale for study, reviewers on, 89
Reason, P., 49
Recruitment & Retention in Higher Education, 14
reference list, for journal articles, 91
regression analysis, 28, 82–83, 84
reliability
   in data collection tool, 73
   in qualitative research, 60
Renaissance College, University of New Brunswick, 52
report. See also manuscripts; research results
   in qualitative research, 60–61
representativeness of sample, 74, 75, 76, 92–93
research, assessment vs., ix–x, 91–92
research databases, accessing and using, 7–11
research design, 45–46, 77–79, 93
Research Into Higher Education Abstracts, 10
research participants. See participants, research
research question. See also framing the question
   dependent variable and primary independent variables and, 69–70
   development of, ix–xii, 2–3
   interviews and, 54
   purpose of study and, 35–36, 36*f*
   researcher approach and, 50–51
   revealed by substantive literature review, 14–15
   write-up of, 92
Research Reports on College Transitions, 100
research results. See also manuscripts

dissemination of, 49
    other dissemination outlets for, 97–100
    publishing in academic journals of, 86–87
    reviewers on congruence of discussion, recommendations and, 94
    reviewers on relationship between current and previous studies of, 94–95
    writing articles and reports for disseminating, 85
researchers
    eligibility as, viii–ix
    qualitative, role and disposition of, 43–44
    quantitative, role and disposition of, 64–65
respect, for human subjects, 34
review form, for academic journals, 87
Review of Educational Research, 16
Review of Higher Education, The, 9, 14, 87
Rice, R., 48
Richardson, S., 53
Richardson, S. M., 6
Robinson, W. S., 58
Robson, K., 54
Roderick, C., 52
Roger, P. R., 6
roundtable discussions, at conferences, 99

S
sampling, 73–77, 93
scholarly articles, statement of purpose for, 66
Schwitzer, A. M., 6
scientific method, quantitative research and, 63
secondary data analysis, 31–32, 70–72
Sedlacek, W. E., 6, 55
Senecal, K. S., 56
SENSE (Survey of Entering Student Engagement), 71
Shedding Light on Sophomores: An Exploration of the Second College Year
    (Tobolowsky & Cox), 13
significance of research, reviewers on description of, 95
Silverstein, L. B., 59
size of sample, 74
snowball sampling, 76
social integration, theory of, 5–6
Social Sciences Citation Index, 11

Sociology of Education Abstracts, 11
Special Educational Needs Abstracts, 11
standard deviation, measures of, 79–80
statistical analysis
    academic reviewers on, 94
    methods for, 77, 79–84
    in quantitative research, 28
    by quantitative researcher, 64
statistical modifications to samples, as bias control, 77
stratified random sample, 76
Strauss, A. L., 46
Strayhorn, T. L., 83–84
striving for future-self, 6
structural equation modeling, 82
Student Affairs Today, 14
student agency, better-than-expected-student engagement and, 4
student data, 72
Student Success in College: Creating Conditions That Matter (Kuh, Kinzie, Schuh,
        & Whitt), 101
students in transition
    current theories on, 5–6
    research on, viii
students in transition movement, age of, vii
subjects. See participants, research
substantive literature, 12–15
Sullivan, M. M., 6
survey instruments
    interviews and, 53–54
    limited, 55–56
    for quantitative research, 28, 73
Survey of Entering Student Engagement (SENSE), 71
Suskie, L. A., 73

T

tables, for journal articles, 90, 94
targeted sampling, 76
Teaching Professor, The, 14
technical writing, of quantitative researchers, 65
Terenzini, P. T., 56
text-based data, in qualitative research, 24

textual analysis, 56–57
Theory Into Practice, 10
theory
    critical, as approach to qualitative research, 47, 48–50
    current, on students in transition, 5–6
    of journal articles, 90
    role in research for, 3–4
Thomas, M., 54
Tieu, T.-T., 66–67
timeline for research, 32–33, 49
Tinto, V., 5, 51
title of manuscript, 87–88
topics, for research, 2
Torres, V., 20
t-tests, 81–82, 84
Tuttle, K., 54
2009 National Survey of First-Year Seminars, 13
2006 National Survey of First-Year Seminars, 13
2003 National Survey of First-Year Seminars, 13

U

universal-diverse orientation, 6
University of New Brunswick, Renaissance College at, 52
Upcraft, M. L., 12

V

validity, 60, 72–73
variables, in quantitative research, 67–70
variance, measures of, 79–80
verbs, research question, 36, 36*f*
Voelker, J. C., 73–74

W

W questions, in research, viii–xii, 2–3
Wabash National Study of Liberal Arts Education, x
Web of Science, 11
Weissman, J., 66, 82
Western Interstate Commission for Higher Education, xii

wikis, for publishing research results, 97
Williams, J. M., 2
Wilson Library Bulletin, 8
Windschitl, M., 55
Wolcott, H. F., 46, 51
Wolf-Wendel, L. E., 54
WorldCat, 7
writing
    for academic periodicals, 100
    by qualitative researchers, 43
    by quantitative researchers, 65
    reviewers on, 89–90

Y
Your First College Year (YFCY) survey, x, 71